Train Your Dog
the Easy Way

Train
Your Dog
the Easy Way

Danny & Sylvia Wilson

Sterling Publishing Co., Inc.
New York

The authors and the publisher do not accept any
responsibility for any loss, damage, injury or inconvenience
sustained by any person or any pet as a result of using the
methods outlined in this book.

Library of Congress Cataloguing-in-Publication data available

2 4 6 8 10 9 7 5 3 1

Published 1996 by Sterling Publishing Company, Inc.
387 Park Avenue South, New York, N.Y. 10016

Originally published in Australia in 1996 by
Lansdowne Publishing Pty Ltd, Sydney

Distributed in Canada by Sterling Publishing
c/o Canadian Manda Group
One Atlantic Avenue, Suite 105
Toronto, Ontario, Canada M6K 3E7

Printed and bound in Singapore by Kyodo Printing Co Pte Ltd

Sterling ISBN 0-8069-9499-1

About the authors

Danny and Sylvia Wilson have had 25 years' experience in animal handling, and are much in demand as dog behavioral therapists. They met soon after Danny moved to Australia from the United Kingdom—one of the first places he visited was an RSPCA animal shelter where Sylvia was the manager.

They found they had much in common—their mutual attraction, their love of and expertise with animals, and their frustration at seeing dog owner after dog owner leave their wayward charges at an overtaxed facility. This led them to form Bark Busters, which is now the largest dog training organization in Australia, and is also rapidly growing internationally.

Danny and Sylvia Wilson have produced many videos, on topics such as teaching children how to interact safely with dogs, and training government employees to prevent harassment or attack by strange dogs. They have trained dogs for movie, theater and farm work, and are often invited by dog enthusiasts to lecture on dog behavior.

Danny Wilson is the author of the best selling *Curing Your Dog's Bad Habits*.

FOREWORD

Ask not what to do for your dog—but what you want your dog to do for you!

Okay, so it's not an entirely original thought. But, after nearly 20 years with the media as a reporter/producer, I thought I'd seen, heard and reported on just about every "new" approach to everyday problems. Then I met Danny and Sylvia Wilson. In one short lesson I watched them cure two barking, out-of-control, food-aggressive spaniels.

Although I watched and videotaped the entire session (which was later broadcast on Australia's Seven Network program *11AM*), for the life of me I couldn't work out exactly how they did it.

Somehow, Danny and Sylvia seemed to know a split second before the dog itself that an attack, involving lightning-fast, bone-crunching bites, was about to occur. Those teeth never connected with flesh, the barking was halted, the dogs walked calmly on leads, and within an hour the eternally grateful owner was well on the way to being able to exert similar control.

How do they do it? Well, to put it simply, Danny and Sylvia Wilson have unraveled the secrets of doggy body language. They're the Allan Pease of the dog world! (I'm referring to the human body language expert and author of several books on how to control others by understanding their gestures well enough to read their thoughts.)

Now, at long last, the Wilsons have explained the techniques I couldn't fathom—in this book. I couldn't put down *Train Your Dog the Easy Way*, because at long last it became clear to me what makes dogs tick, and how we humans can easily take advantage of our knowledge of doggy protocol in order to be in command.

Also, as you will discover, it's fun to read about the classic mistakes we make when training dogs—and to realize how easily they can be corrected with Danny and Sylvia's simple methods. I wish they'd written this book years ago!

Which brings me back to my opening line about what we want from our canine pals. We want a dog that's happy and well adjusted because it knows exactly what is and isn't acceptable to us, and exactly where it fits into the "pack" that inhabits its particular home.

I can't help but think that the more we know about communicating with dogs, the less chance there is of us, and especially our children, being accidentally bitten by them.

So, with Danny and Sylvia's book in hand, I'm off to practice my new-found knowledge on my new puppy, Kismet, in the hope that she'll be less confused than her older playmate Cosmo—who, at 18 months of age, will be learning that older dogs really can be taught new tricks!

Kaye Browne   Freelance TV Producer/Writer

Meeting Danny and Sylvia Wilson was a real eye-opener for me, not to mention what it did for our German shepherd, Beowulf. Beo is three and a half years old, and has been the boss of our house all his life.

I was introduced to the Wilsons and their philosophy through my daughter Tracey, a journalist who'd met them while doing a story. She called me that same day to say, "Dad, you've just got to see what these guys can do. You won't believe it. And it's so simple!"

I was, to put it mildly, highly skeptical. After all, I'd owned and trained four German shepherds over the years, so I was something of an expert, right?

Beo has never really been a problem. He just pulls me all over the place when we're out walking, and takes off after dogs, cats, birds, and, for reasons known only to himself, white Toyota vans. If I don't let go of the lead I get dragged along the grass.

Well, guess what? In just 15 minutes Danny and Sylvia changed it all. Beo is a new dog. He now walks with me, with or without the lead, and he never leaves my left side. He is continually looking at me, waiting for his next command. He was always a beautiful dog; he's just better now.

Danny and Sylvia said that I must get my dog's respect. Well, I have that now. But, more importantly, the Wilsons have mine.

Thank you Danny, and Sylvia.

Philip Curro   Dog Owner

CONTENTS

ABOUT THE METHOD

A "new-wave" dog training technique, our method has been developed after decades of close observation of dog behavior and hands-on training experience. Its aim is to help you communicate with your dog in a language that it can understand.

The language of communication

This book emphasizes the importance of using the language dogs will understand best—and this applies both to body language and to the spoken word.

Most human body language has the opposite meaning to the body language that dogs use. These differences may confuse the dog, and cause difficulty in training. If, for example, a pup jumps up excitedly on you, you may push it down again, using both hands and rapid body movements. The pup is likely to interpret this as a signal to play.

If you use a harsh verbal reprimand at the same time, the pup will be even more confused. Your mixed messages are likely to result in a dog that will jump at people, and then dart away playfully to avoid the ensuing reprimand.

Train Your Dog the Easy Way shows you how to use both body language and spoken language that your dog will understand.

Most training techniques are based on human language, used in the form of verbal commands to a dog. This may be ineffective, however, as dogs will never actually be able to understand our language, and it will take time for them to develop an association between a certain word and a particular action.

With all of these factors in mind, we have developed a one-word command technique, based on both the sounds and actions that dogs make when communicating. By first conditioning a dog to respond to this word, you can teach it to walk correctly in minutes. Basic training will take only a number of hours, followed by a small amount of maintenance.

The training environment

We also believe in the importance of training a dog primarily in its own environment, rather than in territory that is foreign to it, such as a training school. We have discovered that being in an unfamiliar area will cause stress in a dog and distract it, and this will diminish its capacity to learn.

If, however, a dog feels settled in an environment, its retention and its enthusiasm for learning will be increased.

This does not mean that you cannot train your dog in a park or on a training ground at a later stage. But you will find that initially it will be less distracting for the dog to be in its own surroundings, and it will concentrate better because of this—and learn more quickly.

Pack law: understanding dogs

If you want to train your dog effectively, you will also need to understand its nature—that is,

the basic character of the dog. What you need to realize is that, first and foremost, dogs are pack animals. This simply means they are not solitary animals: if they had a choice, they would rather live with others (dogs or humans) than live alone. And, whether their pack consists of other dogs or of people, one of these pack members should be a strong leader.

Much has been written by dog experts about pack instinct, pack law and being the alpha dog (which simply means the "number one" dog). There is hardly a book on dog training that does not mention the subject—so much so, that many people are becoming confused, and are at a loss as to how they should apply the philosophies of pack law and pack instinct to their own dogs.

Why do these concepts seem so complicated to dog owners? We believe the reason for this is that people are trying to understand in their own terms the inner workings of a creature that thinks and reacts wholly differently than humans do. Unless you understand the basic differences between humans and dogs, you will continue to worry about this subject—without any success. (There is much talk these days about the principle of positive reinforcement, sometimes used in human education, and the need to use only this principle when training dogs, without any form of punishment or reprimand. However, as you will see in this book, rewarding a dog for what it has done right is not enough. You also need to show it what it has done wrong—that is, what is unacceptable to you as its leader.)

To help you to understand what principles will work when you are training your dog, we will now explain just what it means for a dog to be a member of a pack.

Pack law made simple

Even though dogs have been domesticated for thousands of years, they still live by the same basic laws as their predecessors in pre-domestication times.

When dogs lived in packs, each pack was ruled by the most dominant dog; this could sometimes be a female. To determine which dog was the most dominant, the pack assessed certain qualities such as body language, strength of character, ability to dominate, and bodily strength (demonstrated in fighting prowess). Pups in the pack would test their muscles, so to speak, with other pups—so much so that most dogs already had a good idea, by the time they reached adulthood, of who their most dominant contemporary was.

In the pack, a dog lacking fortitude would never be the leader (unlike some of the households we see today, where a cowardly dog often rules the roost!). To have such a weak character for a leader would have been fatal to the continued strength of the pack, as in most cases only the pack leaders would mate. And of course it was desirable for the pack's offspring to have those genes that were most favorable to the continuation of a strong pack—strong both in nature and in physical attributes.

The most dominant dog, the leader, would lead the hunt and eat first (followed by the next most dominant dog, and so on). This would guarantee that the health and other attributes of the pack leader and those of its mate would be passed on to the offspring. If the leader always ate first and was well nourished, it was assured of being fit and strong, and of being able to provide its offspring with good nourishment. This would mean the offspring had more chance of being fit and strong too.

A pack leader would very rarely lead for life. The reason for this was that, as it aged, it would be challenged by stronger and younger dogs coming up through the ranks and waiting for a shot at the top job.

These younger dogs would know when it was time to challenge for leadership, because an ageing dog would start to become inconsistent, and display body language that the pack would instinctively recognize as such. An example of a leader's inconsistency would be the practice of backing away from a confrontation one day and then facing it head-on the next.

Such inconsistency would ring alarm bells in the other dogs' minds, warning them that all was not well with their leader. They would soon realize that it was time to launch a challenge for the top job (which is no different from what happens in our corporate dog-eat-dog world!).

Pack law—you and your dog

As tough as pack life may sound, it was the law that the dog would always instinctively follow. And even domesticated dogs today follow the same laws and have basically the same instincts as their forebears, as well as similar instinctive responses to many things. (An example of this is the way a dog's hair will still bristle when it is afraid. Humans, too, have the same kind of instinctive response: we can feel the hairs standing up on the back of our necks when something frightens us.)

There are other distinct parallels between dogs and humans, such as the way we set up challenges for ourselves in order to attain what we strive for in life. For example, both dogs and people often give themselves the challenge of striving to be the leader, the "top dog"—either as leader of the pack, or as chief executive of an organization.

But the most important thing to understand about dogs is that they really want only one thing out of life: to have a pack leader that is consistent and fair. And, for domesticated dogs, that leader may be either another dog or the human owner.

If you can understand this, you will also understand how to establish the most effective relationship possible with the dog you own. You will realize that you have to meet its need for a leader, and that you will fail if you show you are not dominant, act inconsistently, or "over-humanize" the dog. When we treat a dog as if it is human, we stop thinking about it as an animal that is driven by definite and predictable instincts. And we make life more difficult for ourselves by doing so!

If you do any of these things—reveal your lack of dominance, treat your dog as if it is human, or act inconsistently in terms of what you expect from the dog and how you react to certain situations—it may challenge you for the top job. Training it will then be difficult.

Using food as a training aid

Although food is sometimes used as a basis for training, we believe that training a dog in this way will not make for success, because your method will not be meeting the dog's need for a pack leader.

The mere act of feeding a dog because it has completed an exercise, or of showing it that it can only eat once you yourself have eaten, will not turn you into its leader. If this were the case, a pack leader in the wild would only have to be a good provider in order to hold the top position, regardless of what strength of character or degree of dominance it displayed.

The only time you should look to using food for training is as a distraction. For example, if your dog becomes paranoid about a specific place or object, then, by feeding it regularly in that place or near that object, you may overcome its paranoia.

The other time you can successfully use food to help in training is when you are teaching your dog to do tricks (discussed in Chapter Six).

Chapter One

Getting your pup off to a good start

Successful training nearly always depends on having a pup with a suitable temperament. A pup that is confident, friendly and amiable is going to be easier to train than a nervous, anti-social, stubborn one. In this chapter, we will explain how to ensure that you get the right puppy—one whose temperament makes training an easy process.

Do not despair, however, if you already have a pup that is showing temperament problems. You will also find the training methods described in this book suitable for your difficult pup.

Finding the right pup

The best—and the only foolproof—way of finding a pup with the right temperament for your needs is by using a registered, well-established breeder. Breeders who are intent on breeding top-quality, show-winning stock are more likely to be breeding dogs with good temperaments than are dog owners who have decided to breed using their own male and female dogs, or their own dog and a dog belonging to a friend.

The novice breeder would be unlikely to have a good understanding of what a dog with a good temperament is all about. In our experience, such breeders are often motivated more by the physical appearance of the dog or by possible financial gain than by considerations of temperament. (There are no hard and fast rules, of course. Many dogs with a beautiful temperament may come from an inexperienced breeder, but they will be the exception rather than the rule.)

If you decide that you will be getting your pup from a breeder, you will be creating a situation where you can view the parents of your prospective pet. And you will find that meeting the parents of your pup is a bit like meeting the parents of your partner for the first time—it gives you an insight into how your chosen one might turn out.

If one of the parents of your prospective pup has a temperament problem—aggression, shyness or over-exuberance—the possibility is fairly high that this trait has been passed on to the offspring. For obvious reasons, then, you should avoid the pups of such a dog, regardless of how cute they may seem.

The easiest way to select the right pup is to ask the breeder to choose one that is not shy, overly dominant or stubborn. However, if the breeder prefers you do the picking, try to take an experienced person with you to view the pups.

If all else fails, the following tips on getting the right pup should help you.

Selection tips

Watching a group of pups at play will help you to choose the one you want. So, if you do get the opportunity to view several pups, try to arrange to see the whole litter together. Then you will be able to see temperament differences in action. If, for example, you wish to avoid owning a pack-leader type, you can look out for the classroom-bully-type pup that dominates and picks on the other pups. Once you have distinguished this type of pup, you will know that it will not be going home with you!

Likewise, avoid the pup that runs and hides when the bully appears. A pup that barks at you or the other pups should also be avoided at all costs. You do not want a pup that is overly vocal: if one of the litter is barking at this early stage, it is going to be a nuisance barker. Good watchdogs do not usually start barking until they are between seven and 12 months.

Preparing your pup for training

It is vital that you start your puppy's training as soon as it settles down in to your home environment.

A puppy would, as a matter of course, receive discipline and a form of training from its mother and other members of the family, and even its siblings, depending on its position in the pack. So, when you discipline your pup correctly, the way its mother would, you will be filling a void.

As we have already seen in "About the Method", a pup would feel more at ease as part of an ordered pack. A lack of discipline would only unbalance its instinctive behavior.

Using effective spoken language

To discipline and train a pup effectively, you first need an effective form of communication—and speaking to your dog as you would to another person will not get you anywhere. Many dog owners tell us that their dog fully understands everything they say to it. Our answer to this is, "Tie your dog up, and, as soon as it starts barking, write down everything it says." It stands to reason, after all, that as we are far more intelligent than our dogs, we should be able to understand everything they say!

Too many new puppy owners expect far too much from their little charges in terms of what they are able to understand. To be effective, the language used for puppy training must be short and simple.

It is well known that a human baby simply cannot understand language until about six months of age, and at that age will grasp only the very basics. So we cannot expect a creature that has no concept of our language ever to understand it fully— particularly if this creature is an animal that can only communicate with growling, barking and guttural sounds.

However, dogs can relate to voice tones, provided the tone matches the accompanying gesture. The growl is already recognizable to a dog as a reprimand, and is a natural part of its vocabulary, being the sound its mother or litter mates would make when all was not right. Therefore a guttural growl sound, uttered when your pup does something you don't want it to do, followed by a soft, pleasant sound as soon as it stops doing the wrong thing, is all that is needed in most cases.

In our research we have found that the commonly used word "No" is not suitable as a dog reprimand. It is widely used mainly because it is more acceptable to humans than a growl sound, being far more pleasant to human ears. This would be fine—if we were training humans! The problem is, it means nothing to the dog, and is largely ineffective due to the rounded sound the word makes. It is impossible to make an effective growl using the word "No."

Don't make your pup's collar too tight. You should be able to get two fingers under it with ease. Check the collar regularly—pups grow very rapidly.

The fastest and easiest way to accustom your pup to wearing a collar is to put it on each time the pup is eating. In this way, the collar will have very pleasant associations!

When you first put your pup on the lead, let it take you where it chooses. After a few days, start leading it yourself. If the pup resists, crouch down, pat your leg, and talk to it encouragingly.

The "Sit": With your dog on your left, grip the lead with your right hand close to its neck. Gently press on its rump with your left hand. Say "Sit", and release the pressure as soon as the dog sits.

The "Stay": Once you are confident your dog will stay in one place, remove the lead. Remain close to the dog, and use the one-word reprimand if it moves.

The "Drop": Left hand, fingers splayed, on your dog's back; index and middle finger of your right hand on its muzzle and the hand partially covering its eyes. The dog will drop its head as it tries to see under your hand—and its body will follow.

The "Recall": With this exercise, never chase your dog. Stop and crouch as it runs toward you, speaking in an inviting tone. Use the command "Come"—its name alone will not bring it to your side. Praise it lavishly when it comes to you.

The correct words to use when reprimanding are "Bad" or "Bah." Either word, uttered in a growling, guttural voice, will usually get an immediate response. Then, if the dog reacts correctly, follow with a softly encouraging "Good dog."

Remember, too, that your puppy does not understand our language. Therefore, it is unfair to expect it to understand long strings of speech. Talking in long sentences will only slow the learning process down. You need to keep all communication simple: use the same principle as you would if you were teaching a small child how to speak English. For example, you would not start by using long sentences such as, "This is the table where we sit when guests come for dinner." You would be more likely to point at the table and say, "Table."

To help your pup learn quickly, you should therefore choose your reprimand word as suggested. Once you have chosen it, stick to it, and use only that word when you give a reprimand. Do not use it as part of a longer command you are giving the pup. This way it will catch on more quickly.

Using effective body language

As we mentioned in "About the Method", your body language may have as much of an effect on the dog you are training as the spoken language you are using. In some cases, it may have even more impact than your speech.

For example, a dog will sometimes ignore a reprimand if it is given by an owner who is in a crouch, or another position inferior to its own—say, sitting on a couch or standing on a lower stair than the dog.

There are two main reasons it would ignore you in a situation like this. The first is that, with your height lowered, you are in a less commanding position than the dog itself. The second is that you are now in a different position from the one you normally adopt while you ask your dog to respond to a particular command. Dogs only learn by association. For example, if you tend to wear a particular scarf every time you go out to feed your dog, it will eventually become excited whenever it sees that scarf, associating it with feeding time.

Therefore, if you change your usual stance while giving your dog a command, it may not associate this command with the same command given previously.

When, in a situation like this one, a dog does not respond to a command, the owner may mistakenly believe that it is being stubborn or defiant. The truth is, it is the owner's body language that is confusing the dog.

Hands off!

As you have seen, if it is used correctly, your voice can be a very effective training tool. And it is far more useful than your hands.

Because dogs don't have hands themselves, they find any form of discipline by humans that involves their hands both provocative and threatening. So you should never bully, smack or grab your pup. A pup that is regularly grabbed or smacked is likely to start biting its owner to stop this type of discipline.

It goes without saying, then, that you should use your hands as little as possible when you are training your dog. And, if you do use them, this should be only for gentle manipulation

(placing your pup in a sitting or "drop" position), or patting. Your hands must always be associated with gentleness, and with pleasurable experiences.

Using a collar and lead

A collar and lead are two very important items both for a dog and its owner. All pups should be introduced to them early. And a calm, non-traumatic introduction is vital if you want your puppy to love them.

Timing is important too. One of the best ways to introduce the collar and lead is at mealtimes. Firstly, fit a firm-fitting leather or webbing collar, one that is not overly thick or large, on the pup. Make sure that you can comfortably fit two fingers under the collar once it is done up (see page 19).

Attach the lead to the collar, then feed your puppy. Do this every day for a week, constantly extending the time you leave the collar on. A quick and easy method for getting your pup used to its collar and lead is to feed it its favorite "tidbit," but only immediately after you have put the collar on. The idea is that the pup will associate the collar with something pleasurable (see page 19). Never leave a pup that is on a lead unattended during this period, as it could get it caught around objects.

Another way to introduce the collar and lead is during playtime: before starting to play with your pup, put its collar on. The best games with a lead are those where the pup chases either a ball, a toy, or you. As with the food technique, accustom the pup to the collar first, then the lead, and let the lead trail behind the pup. Be sure the area you are playing in is clear of trees and other objects that may snag the lead and frighten the pup.

Tug-of-war games are less desirable, but acceptable if the pup has its own tug-of-war toys. Using your own towels or clothes could create problems for you later, as your pup might come to think it is fun to grab your things.

(You should never play games where you chase the pup around or use your hands to push and wrestle. These types of game may create handling problems later: every time you try to touch the pup it will think it is playtime.)

It is not a good idea to fit a check chain at this early stage, as the sound it makes could frighten the uninitiated pup. The noise may be too dramatic for the pup to cope with, and could traumatize it for the rest of its life. The check chain can be introduced later, once your pup is used to wearing something around its neck.

Once your pup is happy with the collar and lead, it is time to take hold of the lead and allow it to take you for a walk in your backyard (see page 19). This will reduce the amount of trauma it will suffer. Only walk for about five minutes a day, and do this for three days. Always remove the lead once the time is up. Never leave a lead on a pup that is unattended. The lead may be caught on a branch or a chair leg, causing the pup to believe that it is something to be feared.

If you use these basic techniques, which are simple to apply and are based on an understanding of the dog's nature, you will find your pup is well prepared to start its training.

The early basics: preparing for independence

During the early stages of your pup's life—for about the first six months—it will be very dependent on you, and seem quite devoted.

However, this situation will change once the pup is about seven months old. This is usually the age at which pups become more adventurous and more independent, although, of course, this stage will vary from pup to pup, depending on each one's temperament and degree of confidence. In general, though, most pups start to disobey or challenge their owners around this time.

This is mainly due to the dog's pack instincts, and follows the pattern of behavior it would have shown in the wild as a member of a pack. As the young pack dog matured, it became less and less dependent on its mother, and started to prepare itself for adulthood. It had to fit into an established hierarchy, and wanted to work out just how high up the ladder it could climb.

It is these instincts that will drive your pup when the time comes for it to start testing its independence. The early basics of training are therefore very important. If you can establish good ground rules while your pup is still dependent on you and more amiable than it will be later on, then you are halfway to having a well-trained, well-adjusted dog.

Once you have lead-trained your pup, as described above, you can advance fairly quickly. It is, however, just as important to have control off the lead as on the lead, and the best place to start ensuring this is in your backyard.

As mentioned in "About the Method", a pup will learn much faster in its own environment. Besides, a familiar environment means fewer distractions. Distractions will become important later on in your dog's training, but initially they may hamper it.

By now you will have selected a reprimand word, and will be using it regularly. As mentioned above, "Bah" or "Bad," uttered in a guttural, growling voice, are best. "No" is more widely used in dog training, but, as explained, will not immediately be recognized by the dog as a reprimand. The only time a dog comes close to making a sound similar to "No" is when it is howling.

Once your dog is used to both the lead and the reprimand word, it is time to begin the basic training.

"Sit stay" when feeding: good table manners

Good eating habits should be established early if you want to avoid major problems in the future. We are regularly asked for advice by dog owners who find that their dog becomes aggressive if they approach it while it is eating.

This behavior is quite a normal instinct in some dogs—they are only behaving the way they would in the wild, where protecting one's food is vital for survival. However, the same behavior is unacceptable in human society, and we have to teach this to our dogs.

The best way to help your pup learn the acceptable behavior right from the begin-

ning is to show it that you have no desire to steal its food. You can do this by conditioning. Every time you feed your pup, make it sit as soon as you approach with the food. It may be necessary to put a lead on your pup at such times. Then place the food on the ground, and wait about 30 seconds. If the pup tries to move toward the food, say "Bad" or "Bah" in a growling voice, stepping on the lead at the same time. This will prevent the pup from getting to the food before you want it to. If the pup sits, this is good, but it is not important exactly what it does at this early stage—as long as it does not rush at the food.

Praise your pup as soon as it responds correctly. Always release the pressure on the lead as soon as it stops rushing toward the food.

Use the word "sit" as a command for the dog to adopt that position, and "stay" to let it know you want it to stay put. Once you are happy that your pup has the idea and is waiting for permission to move, say "Free," and encourage it to go and eat. Praise it, saying "Good dog" as it does.

Another method you can use is to lift the food off the ground with your right hand as soon as the pup moves toward it and growl, using your reprimand word; again, step on the lead to prevent any forward progress by the pup. Then put the food back on the ground. What you are teaching the pup here is that, every time you bring it food, there are certain manners it has to display. This is really not unlike the way you would teach a child to behave at the dinner table!

Be sure to follow the same ritual every time you feed your pup, and reinforce the correct behavior. As we mentioned in "About the Method" in our description of the pack leader, inconsistency on your part will cause confusion.

Consistency is vital when you are training your dog. It will assure the dog that you are a good leader, and will meet its need for an ordered life.

An excellent sense of hearing

Note that dogs have excellent hearing, and can hear you quite well if you whisper. However, when you are teaching your dog an exercise for the first time, you will need to raise your voice in order to gain its attention. Once the dog is more focused on you, you can then use a lower growl tone to reprimand it, and it will still respond.

Using the correct words

We feel it is important to point out here that the words we suggest as commands—"Sit," "Stay," "Come," "Free," and so on—are chosen because they are words that are not used very regularly in normal, everyday conversation. The story of Clyde and Clara illustrates how important it is to choose carefully the words you use when training your dog, and then use them consistently.

Preventing bad habits

In our experience, bad habits in dogs are undesirable habits that they were allowed to form at an early stage as pups, and were

CLYDE AND CLARA'S CONFUSION

We were once approached by a dog owner who had already started training his two dogs himself, but felt he needed some help. Both dogs, Clyde and Clara, were not remaining in the "sit" or "stay" positions when they should have.

We asked the owner to place Clyde and Clara one by one in a "sit" stay," and we called out certain instructions to him, such as, "Place your dog in a sit," "Leave it," and so on.

His answers to all of our instructions were always the same: "Okay."

And each time he called out to us, his dogs would move from the "sit".

The owner was becoming very frustrated—until we pointed out the problem. The dogs were only responding to the command "Okay," which was exactly what he had taught them! This man had the habit of saying "Okay" each time he released his dogs from the "sit" or "stay". They took this word as a sign that they had already done what they should!

We learn from their story that it is important to choose command words carefully, ones that are not used too frequently in everyday speech. All of the words used in this book for training are those words that the dog will normally hear only during the training process.

then allowed to continue without correction from their owners. Habits become entrenched before you know it—and then need major behavior modification training in order to be corrected.

However, if you get your dog to adhere to certain rules while it is still a pup, you can prevent many bad habits from manifesting themselves—recall problems, biting, mouthing, barking aggression, and so on.

Preparation for the "recall"

It is important to do some preparation while your dog is still a pup if you want to ensure that, as a grown dog, it will respond immediately when you call it to come to you. To introduce the pup to this concept, whenever you are playing with it, or just spending time with it, always make a big fuss every time it approaches you. Pat it and praise it, but never grab or chase it. In the next chapter, we will explain in detail how to train your dog to come when called.

The hide-and-go-seek method

The hide-and-go-seek technique is designed to teach your pup to be more attentive to you. If you teach it this technique correctly, you will cause it to think, "If I don't keep my eye on my owners, they might disappear." We have used this technique with all of our dogs, and as a result they are far more focused on us than most other dogs we have observed with their owners.

The idea is to select a place that is not near a busy roadway. Take your pup to this area, and allow it to investigate the scene. (It must be pointed out here that, if you wish to take your pup to an area away from your home, it should first be fully vaccinated. A dog that has not been immunized against distemper, etc., is at risk of contracting a disease. If in doubt about your pup's readiness to venture out into the world, ask your veterinarian.)

Once your pup is happily sniffing and investigating the new scene, pop behind a tree or hedge, and hide. Be sure that while you are concealed you can still keep an eye on the pup, but it cannot see you.

Some pups will panic immediately if they cannot see their owners. If this happens, do not delay: step back into view and call your pup: "Rex, come." Make a big fuss of it as soon as it reaches you.

Other types of pups could not care less if you disappear. Being allowed to roam may be paradise to them, and they will sniff and forage to their heart's content. With this kind of pup, you will need to call out, and then wait for it to start charging about trying to find you. Next, show yourself, and praise the pup as soon as it comes to you. Here again it is important to say the dog's name, followed quickly by "Come."

Using the dog's name alone when calling your dog is not sufficient. We regularly come across people who use only their dog's name when calling it, and then wonder why the dog does not respond. We show them how fruitless this can be by demonstration: we just call the owners' names, over and over. They stand there, saying "Yes" each time they are called. What they have not realized until now is that, if we call a person using his or her name alone, that person cannot possibly know what we want— least of all that he or she should now jump up and come running to us. It is no wonder that their dogs will not come to them when they call!

Keep two other principles in mind when using the hide-and-go-seek method on your pup. Chasing your pup will teach it to run away from you: it will think it is enticing you into playing a game. Also, do not use your hands to try to restrain the dog. As previously discussed, when you are training your dog your hands should be associated only with positive actions, such as patting the dog.

Reticent Rover—see his story on page 30—could have become aggressive, and could have tried to bite his owner to prevent the owner from grabbing him. The situation could very easily have produced a dog that would launch an attack at the mere suggestion that a reprimand was about to come from its owner.

Rover's story has shown us the danger of using our hands to deal harshly with our pups; the next case history also shows how a mishandled dog can start to retaliate.

How would we react if someone kept hitting us every time we did something wrong? Like Bonnie in the story on page 31, it would not be long before we too became aggressive.

ROVER LOSES HIS RETICENCE

We were called in to help a man who had just purchased Rover, a six-week-old Rottweiler pup, and was having problems getting the dog to come to him. During our interview at the owner's home, we discovered that the pup had been unwilling to approach him from day one.

We asked many questions, trying to find the answer to this puzzle: "Was the breeder an aggressive person?" "Did your pup have any bad experiences when it arrived at its new home?" Each time the answer was "No." The owner told us that, in his opinion, the pup was already a problem when he bought it.

Because we had not yet viewed the pup, our first thoughts were that it had some severe psychological problem. In our experience, even the most timid pups will always approach their new owners, as they will normally bond with the owners on the way home. In Rover's case, it was already a week since he had been brought home, and he was still acting the same way: it seemed that no bond had been formed.

However, once we viewed Rover we realized that this was a different thing entirely. We found that he would approach us happily, coming up to the point where we could touch him. Then he would stop, refusing to come any closer, and each time we advanced he would retreat until he was again out of our reach. This pup most certainly did not have psychological problems: a psychologically unstable pup would, more than likely, not have approached us at all.

Another thing we noticed was that, if we crouched down and held out our outstretched hands to the pup's chin, he would allow us to touch it, and also to scratch him there.

However, he just would not let us touch him on the top of his head. We questioned the owner further and discovered that, on the day Rover was brought home, the pup had relieved itself on the owner's living-room floor.

The owner had misguidedly grabbed his new pup by the scruff of the neck, rubbed its nose in its droppings, and thrown it outside. From that day on, the pup would not let either its owner or anyone else get close enough to do this again.

Rover was fully rehabilitated with therapy that involved crouching and gentle reconditioning, to teach him that the hand that had hurt him before would not hurt him again. His problem would not have occurred if only his owner had known the golden rule: You must never use your hands in anger when dealing with your dog.

BONNIE LOSES HER BITE

Bonnie, a 12-month-old purebred English Bull Terrier, belonged to seagoing Captain John and his wife, Angie. Whenever Captain John went away to work, Bonnie became a problem.

She would viciously attack Angie every time her owner scolded her. The attacks had become so violent that the Captain was reluctant to leave his wife alone with the dog.

When we met Bonnie, we found her to be friendly, very affectionate, and well adjusted, with no apparent psychological problems. We found it hard to believe she would ever bite anyone. After a lengthy interview, we asked Angie for a demonstration of what incited the dog to attack. She stood up over the dog in a menacing way, pointed at the door and, using a very aggressive tone, yelled, "Outside!" Immediately Bonnie was transferred into something almost unrecognizable. Growling and snapping, she looked as if she was about to make a vicious attack on Angie.

We told Angie she could stop her demonstration: the reason for the dog's aggression was now very apparent to us. We asked the Captain's wife if she had ever punished the dog by hitting it either with her hands, or some article.

She thought for a moment, and then answered, "Yes, when she was a puppy I used to smack her with a rolled-up newspaper. However, I did stop that when she started being aggressive toward me."

What was happening in Bonnie's case was that she had become fearful of a smack from Angie, and was also associating the harsh tone of her owner's voice and the word "Outside!" with physical punishment. To protect herself, she would begin growling and snapping.

The reason Bonnie never attacked when Captain John was around was that, when he was at home, he was the one who did the disciplining, and his manner was far less threatening to the dog than Angie's. All of the problems arose when Angie was left alone with the dog.

We carefully conditioned Bonnie to a reprimand word, and explained to Angie how to give commands using her normal speaking voice, avoiding provocative body language and using her hands only for praise. Soon the dog ceased her aggressive behavior toward her owner, and a loving relationship developed between them.

All of Bonnie's problems could have been prevented if only Angie had known the correct way to communicate with her dog when it was a puppy.

If you are aware of the types of problem that can arise from incorrect handling and act accordingly, the training will be successful.

Chapter Two

The four basic commands

We have discovered, over the years, that most people do not ask much of their dogs: they ask only that the dog will not embarrass them in public, and that it will obey some basic commands.

Basic training

What people require of training is that it will produce a dog that fits into their lives without creating any disruption. They want a dog that will come when it is called, sit while they groom it or give medication, lie down on command when it enters the house, and stay on a certain spot if required.

Most people also do not want to spend weeks achieving these results. Our method—of using the dog's natural way of communicating and conditioning it to understand what we want—is very fast and effective. Here are our easy-to-apply techniques for helping your dog to master the four basic commands. (The photographs on page 20 will help you.) Follow them, and in no time at all you will have your dog fitting into your life with ease.

Teaching the "sit" the easy way

The first thing you should do when teaching your dog to sit is to place it on a lead and a check chain. The correct size of the chain should be about 40 inches (1 m) larger than your dog's neck size. When fitting the chain, open it up to the shape of a "P" while facing the dog (see the diagram on page 35). One thing we would like to remind you about here is that the check chain is not designed to choke your dog. The dog is only meant to react to the sound the check chain makes.

The "sit" is one of the easiest obedience commands to teach a dog. Firstly, place your dog on lead. Holding the lead in your right hand about 4 inches (10 cm) from the dog's neck, place your left hand, using only the thumb and index finger, palm down on the dog's rump. Pull the lead back with your right hand as you gently press down with your left hand. Say "Sit" in your normal speaking voice, releasing the pressure as soon as the dog sits (see page 20).

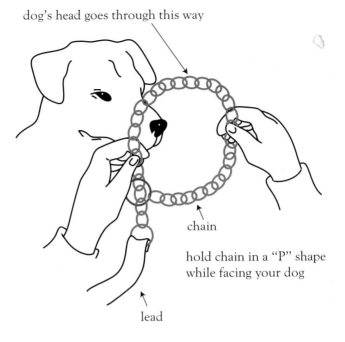

dog's head goes through this way

chain

hold chain in a "P" shape
while facing your dog

lead

Also let the lead out as it does, and remove your hand from its rump. Stand up to your full height slowly, and remain standing in the same position. Do not take any steps away. If the dog stays there, praise it, saying "Good dog" in a very soft, encouraging voice. If the dog moves off the spot, growl your reprimand word—"Bah" or "Bad"—in a loud, harsh tone, and then repeat the "sit"" procedure again, making sure that you growl the reprimand word the second the dog moves, and not before.

A warning: Never leave a check chain on your dog when it is unattended. Many dogs have choked to death when their check chains were caught on a fence or a pole.

Do not rush at your dog or grab it if it moves. You have the lead, so the dog cannot go far. The calmer you remain, the faster your dog will learn. The only time it should hear the reprimand word is at the precise moment it moves— unless it starts to wriggle and try to escape while you are attempting to make it sit.

Then, of course, you would reprimand the dog with "Bah" or "Bad."

Never scold a dog while you are placing it back at the spot where you first left it in the "sit". If, say, you point at your dog and growl, "You naughty dog, do not move," this reprimand will only confuse the dog. Dogs learn by association, and your dog will think it is getting into trouble for sitting.

Remember to keep your commands and reprimands brief and to the point. For example, say, "Sit. Good dog," when your dog obeys you, or "Sit. Bah," when it does not follow your instructions. As we have mentioned earlier, by talking in sentences you will slow down your dog's capacity to learn the exercises quickly, and by reprimanding at the wrong time you will fail to get across to the dog just exactly what it is you do not want it to do—that is, move from the "sit" position.

If you use this "sit stay" technique, described here and in the section below, your dog should take about five to 10 minutes to learn to sit, and then hold that position reliably while you stand beside it. You should therefore keep repeating the exercise for at least five minutes—unless, of course, the dog takes a shorter time than this to show you that it will not move from the spot until you allow it to do so.

Teaching the "stay" command

One of the main reasons for teaching your pup the "stay" command is to make handling it easier—when it is still young, and also when it is a grown dog. Once your dog knows how to "stay", you will no longer have to wrestle with it every time you want to put a lead or collar on it.

If guests arrive at your home, you will be able to make your dog stay in a "sit" or "down" position while they enter. With our own dogs, we try to reinforce this behavior by constant repetition. We use the "stay" command whenever we bring them into or out of our house. The rules are that, as soon as we open any door, the dogs must sit first, and wait until they are invited to come in or go out.

Doing this will help you avoid the common situation of having your dog bolting either into or out of the house as soon as a door is opened. This behavior may become a real problem, as we all find ourselves opening our doors many times a day.

To teach the "stay", put your dog on lead and place it in the "sit", as described in the section above. Then place your hand in front of its face, level with its nose, and say, "Stay." Next, take one big step, turning your whole body to face the dog as you do, and also keeping your eye on it as you move.

This way you will be able to see when to use the one-word reprimand, "Bah" or "Bad," if your dog tries to follow you. Remember, it is important that you reprimand at the precise moment your dog moves, not a little later. A late reprimand will only lead the dog to misread the reason it was reprimanded.

If, for example, your dog moves off the spot and walks over to you and you reprimand it as it reaches you, then it will think it is acceptable to move from the sit—it is just not acceptable to approach you.

So you will need to keep your concentration on your dog as you step away from it, in order to get the correct message through to it.

Be sure to stand up straight and stay put unless your dog moves. If it does, growl your reprimand word. Without rushing or grabbing at the dog, calmly take it back to the spot it moved from. Repeat this exercise over and over until it stays on the spot waiting for you to return to its side.

You can gradually increase your distance from the dog so that you are out of its sight—but ensure that you can see it, so that you can check to ensure that it doesn't move from the "stay".

When your dog has "stayed" for a minute, return to its side, wait a few seconds, and then say "Free." Praise it, and pat it lavishly. It has done what you wanted, and you must reward it.

Daily training is important if you want your dog to respond to your commands, and to adopt the "sit" and "stay" positions whenever you wish it to.

If you start by using only the one-word reprimand, rather than the command you require your dog to follow, it will do the exercise immediately: if it tries to move from the "sit" or the "stay", and you utter the "Bah" or "Bad" word, it will respond to this. Later it will start realizing that the "sit" position corresponds to the command "Sit," and at this stage you can teach it the command word; by this time it will already be doing the exercise correctly anyway, because of its conditioned response to the reprimand word.

Timing

As we have shown above in relation to the "sit" and the "stay" exercises, timing is vital in all obedience exercises if you want to teach your dog both quickly and easily. You must only reprimand at the precise instant the dog moves or does the wrong thing, not after the fact. In order for it to interpret correctly what you want, your dog must be able to associate what it is doing wrong with the reprimand it knows.

Likewise, it must receive praise the instant it does the right thing. Let it know at the correct moment, "This is what I want from you." If your dog looks or acts confused, it is

only because your timing is wrong and it is getting the wrong message.

Teaching the "drop" command

Many people fail to see how having a dog drop on command can be beneficial, but teaching a dog to "drop stay" is one of the most useful things a dog owner can do. For example, it can be a very handy way of controlling your dog when you have guests or while you are eating a meal; it could also save your dog's life in an emergency situation, as you will see when you read Monty's story.

It is not advisable to leave a dog in a "sit stay" position for any length of time. Sitting is a fairly demanding position for a dog; if it sits for too long, it will tire. But you can confidently leave a dog in a "drop stay" for up to 20 minutes, knowing it will be comfortable.

In the past, the "drop stay" exercise was deemed the most difficult for a dog to learn, but this was due, more than anything else, to ineffective techniques.

MONTY AVOIDS MISFORTUNE

One of our first dogs, a German shepherd named Monty, who went on to become an obedience champion, might not have lived a long and happy life if not for the "drop" exercise.

One day, while we were out in a field exercising him, he spotted a rabbit and made chase. It all happened far too fast for us to call him off. By the time we noticed what he was doing, he was well gone.

The rabbit quickly outdistanced him, and managed to cross a very busy road. Monty was now approaching the same road, in hot pursuit. We could tell that there was no way he would make it across safely—a large truck was approaching.

We ran desperately after him, hoping to get close enough to stop the chase. Then we both remembered the "Drop" command, and one after the other yelled "Drop!" as loudly as we could. We waited for what seemed an eternity. Monty was almost at the road now, and all we could do was stand there waiting for the inevitable collision.

Suddenly we saw him skid to a halt, and drop to the ground. Our training had paid off. We both feel sure that, had it not been for the "Drop" command, Monty would have been killed that day.

One such method called for the owner first to make the dog sit, and then to pull out the dog's front legs; this would usually end in a wrestling match. Other methods also tended to involve two separate movements—sitting, then lying.

The method described below, of our own invention, is by far the simplest way to get a dog to drop, and one that creates no stress in the dog—or its owner. It involves dropping from the "stand," which makes the movement smoother and faster, and very appealing to people who enter their dogs in competitions. A fast drop is also vital when you want to stop a running dog in its tracks.

To teach the "drop," have your dog on lead and on your left side. Hold the lead in your left hand, or place it on the ground and step on it, to prevent the dog from moving away from you. Place your left hand on the dog's back, fingers splayed, with your thumb nearest you and with your fingers on the dog's left side. If you are holding the lead, hook the handle onto your thumb and gather the slack under the palm of your left hand as it lies on your dog's back.

Now place the index and middle fingers of your right hand on the dog's muzzle, holding these fingers apart to form an inverted "V". Then rock your dog to both left and right a few times, saying "Drop" (see page 20). If it resists, use the one-word reprimand.

Once the dog starts to move downward, praise it. When it drops to the ground, stand up straight beside it, and be ready to reprimand it if it attempts to stand up without a command

from you. It should remain in the "drop" position until you say "Free."

What makes our technique so effective and so much easier for the dog is that, when you place a hand on its muzzle, it tries to see under your hand, lowering itself and going into a drop naturally. Try this exercise daily, so that eventually your dog will adopt this position every time you say "Drop."

Teaching your dog to come when called (the "recall")

We firmly believe that one of the most important things a dog can learn is to come whenever it is called (the "recall", as we call it). After all, if your dog will not come to you when you call it, trying to teach it any other command will prove useless.

If you have been teaching your dog to come to you as described in Chapter One, then you will already be halfway there. However, it is never too late to teach your dog the "recall." You will require two lightweight leads, one 12 feet (4 m) and one 45 feet (15 m) long. Use the shorter lead in your backyard, and save the longer one for when you venture out to places where you will have more space. Both leads should have a clip, which can be attached to the dog's collar, and a comfortable handle. The idea behind having a lightweight lead is that the dog should not feel the weight of the lead at all.

You can easily make your own leads, with items purchased from your local hardware store. You will need a snap clip, one that is strong and snaps shut automatically. This device should be similar to the connecting clips used by mountain climbers, but of a size suited to your dog. The cord of the lead should be a lightweight rope; we use mower or venetian blind cord. Make a handle out of a leather strap, or pieces of an old handbag. Note that, whatever parts you choose for your leads, they should be both strong and durable.

This exercise should first be tried out in your own backyard using the shorter lead. Then try it in your front yard before venturing out.

Place your dog on the lead, and grip the handle. Walk around the yard with the excess of the lead trailing on the ground. Don't worry if it becomes tangled under the dog's legs—most dogs will manage to step clear. However, if the dog becomes impossibly caught up, stop and untangle the mess.

Each time your dog strides ahead of you or investigates something, tug and then release the lead, and use your one-word reprimand until it turns to move in your direction. Then, still holding onto the lead, let it go slack, crouch down, and call the dog: "Rex, come." Pat your leg to encourage it to come to you (see page 20).

Even though this is a command, it should be delivered in a very pleasant, inviting tone. Once your dog has come to you, pat it as you straighten up to your full height again. Repeat the process several times.

Teaching a distracted dog to come when called

Most dogs will come to their owners when called if there are no other distractions, but once something more interesting is around, such as another dog, a cat, or some food, the owner is fast forgotten. However, it is important that your dog knows it should come whenever called, no matter what is happening around it. Here is the way of ensuring that it is reliable with the "recall."

With your dog still on the lightweight lead, throw its ball or favorite toy. Allow it to chase the toy five or six times and enjoy the game. Then, the next time, stop the dog's progress to its ball or toy by standing on the lead and yelling "Bah!" or "Bad!"

Now crouch, encouraging your dog to come to you by saying its name, and following this with the command "Come," uttered in a soft, inviting voice. Praise the dog as soon as it arrives at your side. If your dog is charging after an object or another animal, you must be able to stop it in its tracks. If you use the reprimand word before the command "Come," the dog will learn the "recall" faster, and will also stop in its tracks much faster. In order to know when to stop, it does not have to hear a complicated set of instructions, just the growl that is already very familiar to it and means it is doing something wrong—something that it should stop doing immediately.

So, if your dog is running away and you yell "Bah!" or "Bad!", it will stop on the spot and return to you. Then, if you use your dog's name, followed quickly by "Come" every time this situation arises, it will eventually learn to "come" on command. In the meantime, while it is learning this command, you will still be achieving the desired result—your dog will come when called whenever you use the one-word reprimand.

If your dog refuses to respond to the reprimand word when you throw its ball, and persists in running after the ball, keep using the reprimand word, and also tugging on the lead. Persist in this, because if you can stop a dog chasing its ball, you will eventually be able to stop it chasing anything. Using this technique will not stop your dog from chasing its ball in the future, as you can vary the training by, say, allowing the dog to chase for six throws of the object, and then stopping it on the seventh throw.

Once you have been using this regular pattern for a while, use an irregular one instead: sometimes allow it to chase the ball only on every second throw, and then at another time stop your dog's progress on the first throw.

Make sure, even as you vary the pattern, to allow the dog many chances to chase, in order to keep its interest in its toy or the ball.

Then repeat the above exercise using food to vary the training; it may also be needed if you have a dog that will not chase a ball or a toy. Just throw the food, sometimes allowing the dog to get it, and sometimes requiring it to come back at the "recall" command.

The reprimand chain

If you have a stubborn dog that refuses to respond to all of your efforts, you will require the use of a reprimand chain. This can be made by purchasing approximately 2 feet (60 cm) of zinc-coated high-tensile steel link chain. The chain is the equivalent of the check chain, and makes a similar sound.

Unlike the check chain, however, the reprimand chain will allow you to reach the dog when it is refusing to respond to your command or reprimand—you can throw the chain so that it falls near to the dog. The dog will usually respond, because of the similar sound this chain makes to the check chain: a reprimand chain, when thrown, sounds the same to the dog as if you were pulling the check chain close to its ear.

Throw the reprimand chain as close to the dog as possible, at the same time yelling "Bah!" or "Bad!" Praise the dog lavishly as soon as it heads in your direction.

Use the techniques described here and, like Bronson in the case history, your dog will respond instantly each time it is called.

BRONSON COMES BACK

One of the worst cases of a dog that would not come when it was called was described to us by its owner. He came to us asking for help with his unruly 12-month-old Border collie, Bronson, who had wreaked havoc at a picnic ground with his bad behavior.

The owner and his family had gone to the picnic ground for the day, taking the dog with them. When the family arrived at their picnicking spot, the children tied their dog to a small picnic basket with his lead, and everyone settled down to have lunch. This worked very well—until Bronson spotted another dog, which was walking past on-lead.

Bronson took off at high speed, trailing the picnic basket and all its contents behind him. The woman walking the dog began to run, trying to avoid a collision as Bronson's family all started running after him, calling to him to come back. Bronson knocked the woman flying as both the picnic basket and his lead whipped her legs from under her. She screamed, and let go of her own dog. It bounded off, startled by its unaccustomed freedom, and Bronson bounded after it, with his own family in pursuit.

All that the family could do was to follow their dog's trail of destruction. They encountered many an angry picnicker, finally catching up with Bronson as he ran between two trees into an opening too narrow for the picnic basket to fit through.

Once we had heard this sorry tale, we showed Bronson's owner and his family how to teach their dog their language by conditioning him with the one-word reprimand. Bronson turned out to be one of the most intelligent dogs we had ever met. He had simply had no idea that his owners did not condone his unruly behavior. Once he had been conditioned, he returned every time he was called.

Chapter Three

Out and about

While some dog owners are able to go out for a quiet walk with their well-behaved charges, others are dragged all over the place by their dogs. Owners' techniques to gain control vary, from digging their heels in and grabbing tree branches as they pass, to wrapping the lead several times around their hands to slow down a dog that is furiously intent on getting to wherever it has decided to go.

Who's the boss?

A dog owner once explained to us his own way of handling the problem of walking his dog—after calling us in to help him teach his dog, Toby, to walk correctly. "When I take Toby for a walk, I place him on the lead, look at him, and say, 'Where are we going to go today, Toby?'"

We have visited many training grounds in our time and seen many different techniques for teaching a dog to walk correctly on the lead and "at heel," as it is commonly known, but we believe that none of these techniques is as quick or as easy as the system which we will describe here.

One reason is that these techniques use the "Heel" command, and this causes a problem right from the start: at the beginning of the exercise, the dog will have no idea at all what the word "heel" means. You may as well be using the word "bananas"!

As we mentioned earlier in this book, dogs do not understand our language. Words in themselves have no meaning to our dogs—they will respond only to the sounds of the words we utter. That is why using a command word when trying to teach a dog to walk correctly may take many weeks.

If you want your dog to learn quickly how to walk correctly on the lead, the one-word reprimand method is the quickest and easiest way. If you are reprimanding as opposed to commanding, the dog will quickly learn that it is wrong to pull. If you praise as soon as the dog stops pulling, it will also learn that it is right to walk calmly at your side.

We can explain this further by using an analogy. Imagine you were walking towards the edge of a cliff in the dark; we know it is there, but you do not.

There are two ways we could save you from disaster. The first would be by calling your name, and saying, "Come over here." We could repeat this each time you approached the cliff edge. Although we haven't told you why we have called you away, eventually you would work out that there was something strange going on because, being human, you can reason things out for yourself.

A dog, not having the capacity of human reasoning, would take a lot longer to work the same thing out and would continue to walk towards the cliff's edge. The command technique would not be telling you—or the dog in a similar situation—anything about the impending disaster.

If, however, I yelled "No!" instead of giving you a command, you would immediately know you were making a mistake and stop. And doing the same thing to your dog—in this case, yelling "Bah!" or "Bad!"—would stop it in its tracks immediately, if it had been taught to respond to the word you were yelling.

That is why using the one-word reprimand method is effective: by now your dog will know the word, and will respond immediately when you use it. Using this method, as well as the correct timing, you will be able to teach your dog to behave safely in any situation. And it will also be easy to teach it to walk along calmly and quickly at your side whenever you need it to.

Teaching your dog to walk correctly on the lead

To start teaching your dog using this method, you will need a check chain that fits it correctly, and a 6-ft (2-m) long webbing lead. Place the dog on-lead. Anchor the lead—that is, secure it tightly—in your right hand, and gather up the slack in your left hand (see page 62).

Now, with your dog on your left side, start walking. Each time the dog pulls ahead, check it by making a backward motion with your left hand. Keep your elbow straight as you do, bending your body forward, and coming momentarily to a halt. Let your hand swing past your body as if you are marching, and then let it make a snap-release action in conjunction with the reprimand word. Then, as the lead becomes taut, immediately release the lead in your left hand. At the same time, growl your one-word reprimand. Praise your dog the moment it responds.

What you should be trying to achieve here is getting the check chain to make the clinking sound that your dog will respond to. Then, once the dog has heard the sound, you will be releasing the lead so that it receives a loose lead—this will discourage the pulling, because your dog is now being checked rather than being able to pull, as it loves doing.

Checking with the chain is a quick movement, a snap-release action: as the dog takes up all of the slack in the lead by pulling, you will again have to slacken it, in order to check the dog. In other words, to get a loose lead, you will have to move your hand forward, and then snap it backward. This is similar to the action of cracking a whip. Checking means, in effect, tightening and releasing the lead in quick succession, always leaving the dog with a loose lead. It is important to keep your elbow straight, and check straight back past your leg (see page 61).

When the lead is loosened, the dog may at first try to run further away from you, but if it is checked it will try to avoid being in the same situation again. The next time the lead is loosened, it will learn to stay at the spot where it does not have to hear the checking sound— right at your side.

Also, if you keep the lead loose, your dog will not be able to feel it, and will therefore not know if it is on- or off-lead. At a later stage, when you are doing off-lead training, you will find it very useful if your dog is already accustomed to the feeling of not being on a lead!

During on-lead training, be sure that you hold the lead loosely and only snap and release quickly, not holding the lead taut for any time at all (see page 61). Holding the lead tightly will only encourage your dog to pull, as dogs are natural pullers. (Just think for a moment of sled dogs, and how they love

JACKSON GETS MORE FROM HIS JAUNTS

Jackson was a Boston Terrier who still could not walk correctly on a lead after 12 months at his local obedience school. We asked the owner to explain how she had been attempting to teach Jackson to walk correctly, and what equipment she was using at the time. She said that her dog club did not believe in steel check chains, and had issued her with a leather-type check chain.

The method she was using to teach the dog to walk correctly was by snapping the lead backward and shouting the "Heel" command. But still Jackson pulled ahead, refusing every effort to get him to walk correctly.

We explained to the owner the purpose of the check chain, and how it really works: the fact is, the chain is not meant to be used to "choke" the dog. A dog reacts only to the sound of the chain, and responds to this when the chain is used correctly. A leather check chain, which makes no noise at all, can only have the effect of choking the dog. And obviously, in Jackson's case, choking did not work, because after 12 months of obedience school training, which meant 12 months of choking and hearing the command "Heel!", he had still learnt nothing.

Using the check chain and the one-word reprimand method, we had Jackson walking calmly at heel in just 15 minutes, and he never reverted to his old habits again.

to pull their burden!) Also, you should avoid using collar and chest harnesses—they will encourage the dog to pull.

Using the method we have described, you should have your dog walking correctly in about an hour—or even less. If you are not getting results, you are probably not using the method correctly. Check your technique, and try again.

In the early stages of training, you will probably need to do minor maintenance, such as reminder checks (check-and-release using the one-word reprimand), each time you take your dog for a walk.

Dogs that over-react to the check chain

A small percentage of dogs will react adversely to the check chain because of its high-pitched sound. However, if the basic training steps in Chapter One are carried out correctly, most dogs will accept this device with time, and your patience will be rewarded.

The check chain is still one of the better training aids available to us today. A certain number of dogs will never accept the chain, but these will be few indeed. And, most often, they will be suffering some trauma as a result of the incorrect introduction of the chain.

We never fail to be amazed at the immense lack of knowledge about how to use the check chain. We are convinced that even the person who invented this chain did not quite know how it should work! The case histories of both Charlemagne and Jackson highlight the importance of introducing the check chain correctly when lead training.

Getting your dog in and out of your motor vehicle

One of the most valuable exercises you can teach your dog is how to enter and alight from your motor vehicle correctly. It should know how to enter the vehicle when instructed, show good manners while sitting inside, and not jump out as soon as you open the door. After all, there will be occasions when you will only be stopping for a moment—say, to get something out of the back of the car.

If your dog has the habit of jumping into your vehicle without being told, then you have a potential problem if it happens to be covered in mud: as soon as you open the door of the vehicle to get something out of it, you may find it appearing from nowhere, jumping in, and rolling about on the upholstery.

THE CHECK CHAIN FRIGHTENS CHARLEMAGNE

Charlemagne, a two-year-old black poodle, had refused from day one to walk on a lead for her owners. They had tried several things themselves, and even called in a professional trainer.

All to no avail. The training by the trainer only seemed to traumatize the little dog further.

When we were called in to treat Charlemagne's problem, we discovered that the check chain was the root of it all. Because of the incorrect introduction of the chain, she now refused to walk with any type of collar on at all. She was suffering long-term psychological problems, and was afraid to take even one step while on lead.

Her owners also had a little male chocolate-colored poodle named Eugene, who loved his walks. But the owners had stopped walking him, because they felt sorry for Charlemagne, who would have had to accompany Eugene each time he was taken out.

We decided that the best treatment for Charlemagne's particular phobia was to loop the "walking lead" through Eugene's collar and then attach it on to hers, a leather collar which we had fitted. We had figured that, if she associated people with her fear of the lead, the best way to get her to walk on lead was to have a dog take her (a dog that, although she did not realize it, was in turn being taken for a walk by its owners!).

So together, much to their owners' delight, Eugene and Charlemagne went off for a walk on lead—and Charlemagne did not protest! Soon they were going for walks daily, with Charlemagne trotting along wagging her tail.

We knew that, in time, once Charlemagne learned to love her walks, her fear of the lead would disappear forever.

To teach your dog good traveling manners, you will need to start by having it on a check chain and lead beside your vehicle. You will be teaching it that it must wait for the "Free" command before it gets into or out of the vehicle.

With your dog on lead, open the door, using the reprimand word if it tries to jump in. Check the dog back at the same time: tighten and release the lead in quick succession, always leaving the dog with a loose lead. (Remember that it is important to keep your elbow straight, and check straight back past your leg.) Then make your dog sit and wait. If it begins to forge ahead, but stops momentarily when you check it and give the one-word reprimand, be sure to voice-praise it. After a couple of minutes, say "Free," and check the dog toward the open door. Praise it as soon as it moves forward. Also give your dog a quick pat each time it moves in the direction you want it to.

Then repeat the same exercise when you are getting the dog out of the vehicle, with one difference: now block the open door

JESSIE JINXES THE JOB

Jessie, a springer spaniel loved to travel with her owner in his car. She was very boisterous and would spring from the back seat into the front seat whenever her owner stepped out of the car for a moment.

One day, Jessie's owner was hurrying to an important business meeting involving a large contract when he discovered that he had forgotten some documents. Rushing back inside, he left Jessie in the car and the engine running.

Leaping and springing about, Jessie stepped on the automatic door lock button, locking all of the doors. Her owner spent a frenzied 20 minutes rushing from one side of the car to the other until she finally stepped on the same button again, unlocking the doors.

Jessie's owner still managed to secure the contract—the client found his story of why he was late very amusing!

with your body. Reprimand with "Bah" or "Bad" as soon as your dog attempts to jump out. Repeat this exercise several times, and always follow the same procedure every time you open the door.

Once you have taught your dog how to enter and exit from your vehicle correctly, you should also teach it how to behave while it is traveling. If you start by teaching the dog to behave in a sensible manner when it first travels with you, then you will find that every time it climbs in it will quickly settle down for a peaceful journey.

One way to establish good behavior in the car is to have either a doggy seat belt (this is available at most pet stores) or an anchor spot to tie your dog to. Be sure to tie the lead fairly short, and to a collar, not a check chain. If you have to leave the vehicle briefly—say, to run in and pick something up—your dog could panic and get tangled. If you do have a dog that panics when you leave it, just hop out of the car for a few moments each time you stop, and then jump back in. This way your dog will start to get used to your leaving.

Attentiveness training

You may be one of those unfortunate dog owners who often laments, "I wish I could make my dog more devoted and attentive!"

The good news is that you can do just that. All you have to do is follow these instructions for a few days. The exercise works well with most puppies, and is also very useful if you have acquired an older dog and are trying to get it to bond with you as quickly as possible.

Attentiveness training requires a lot of open space—you should use a park or a field. You will need your lightweight cord, with a snap lock and handle attached (see page 62).

Holding the cord by the handle only, walk in a straight line, not speaking to your dog. Tug on the lead only if the dog tries to pull in the opposite direction. If it comes rushing up to you or passes you, turn and go in the opposite direction immediately. Then turn again each time your dog comes up to you, or races ahead. The reason for turning constantly is to get the dog to pay close attention to where you are moving to. Some dogs will quickly work out in which direction their owners are going, and then stop concentrating on the person who is walking with them; instead, they will sniff around and investigate the area to their heart's content. However, if you keep on turning each time the dog comes near to you, it will not be able to predict where you are going, and will have to focus fully on you all the time.

Repeat the exercise over and over. Go in different directions each time, and keep extending the distance between you and your dog whenever you do so. If the dog becomes slightly tangled in the lead, keep going. In most cases it will untangle itself. However, if it does become hopelessly caught up, you will have to stop and free it. For a week, do this exercise for about five minutes each day. Eventually your dog will learn never to take its eyes off you and will certainly become much more attentive!

Preparation for walking off the lead

Before you take your dog off-lead you should do some preliminary work. Firstly, when you are walking along with your dog at heel and on-lead, lay the lead over the dog's back and walk along the same way you would if you had hold of the lead (see page 62).

Use your reprimand word if your dog starts to rush ahead or becomes distracted and praise with your voice as soon as it comes back to position.

Continue in this way for the next few days or until your dog reliably stays at heel and you have control using only your voice. You must be confident that your dog will respond to your voice before you take it off lead. Now you're ready to venture out in public with your dog off its lead!

Chapter Four

Off the lead

Being able to control your dog when it is off the lead is not something that happens overnight. However, if you have carried out all of the preliminary exercises discussed in previous chapters, you will be able to progress to off-lead work without a problem.

Controlling your dog

A good way to start gaining control of your dog off-lead is to let it run free, but make it think you still have it on-lead. And the simplest way to do this is to start letting go of the lead when you are in an enclosed park or field.

With the reprimand chain in your hand, allow the dog to stride away from you. Then throw the chain near its back legs, and reprimand the dog, using the one-word reprimand. Next, crouch down and encourage it to come back to you. Praise it as it approaches. Growl the "Bah" or "Bad" word if it stops on the way to you, or deviates from the most direct path in your direction. Repeat this exercise several times until your dog responds immediately you yell the reprimand word.

Now try asking a friend or relative—someone the dog knows—to help you. Have your assistant lead the dog a short distance away from you, keeping it on the lead. Instruct him or her to move approximately 10 feet (3 m) away the first couple of times, and then further and further away as the dog makes progress.

As soon as your assistant has moved away with your dog, throw your reprimand chain so that it lands as close to the dog as possible, and yell the reprimand word. Instruct your assistant to let go of the dog as soon as it responds to your call.

Eventually you will be too far away from your dog to be able to throw the chain anywhere near it, but this does not matter. The sound of the chain will still reach the dog, and it should respond in the same way as it did when the chain was nearby.

A special note: If your dog responds adversely to this exercise—that is, if it panics and tries to run away—stop using the reprimand chain, and use only the one-word reprimand, leaving the lead on the dog until it gains confidence, and seems to understand what you want it to do. A nervous dog will need a great deal of encouragement, which you should give by crouching and praising.

Once your dog is returning to you each time you yell the reprimand word, you may remove its lead and do the same exercises off lead. At this stage you should still leave the check chain on—it is important that you do not remove it, as the dog will not respond as well without it. We have found that, when the dog is off the lead in the early stages of its training, it associates the check chain with the control you had over it while the lead was still on.

Have your assistant lead your dog away by the check chain. Again increase the distance between the dog and yourself, and have your assistant vary the direction in which he or she takes the dog.

If you follow these steps you will find that your dog will eventually refuse to leave your side when it is not on the lead. When this happens, you are well on your way to having a dog that is controllable off the lead.

Teaching your dog to walk correctly off the lead

Once you have gained on-lead control of your dog using the technique described in the previous section, the transition to having the dog walking correctly by your side off-lead will be easy—for both you and the dog. The only condition for success is that you should maintain exactly the same body language as you used in the earlier exercise.

If you have been holding your hands a certain way when grasping the lead, then they must be in exactly the same position when you are doing the off-lead training. There are two reasons for this. As mentioned in Chapter One, dogs learn by association. By seeing you in the same position as you were at an earlier stage, they will respond to you as they did previously. Also, if your hands are in a different position now that the dog is off the lead, it may soon realize that you are no longer holding the lead.

CHOWSIE IS CHASTENED

We remember only too well that day we chased Chowsie. It was the day that our quickly taught technique for recalling dogs saved our skins, and also a little dog's life.

We were asked by a local theater group to select and train a Yorkshire terrier for the stage play Gypsy. We duly found the right dog, a stray that we picked up from the pound, and named him Chowsie, because this was the name of the doggy character in the play.

Chowsie had obviously had no training whatsoever—he would snap at anyone who tried to pick him up. Fortunately, this was a problem that we did manage to solve in time for the show. We conditioned him first with the one-word reprimand, and then accustomed him to being carried everywhere, reassuring him with lots of praise.

Another problem Chowsie had, which was more pressing, was that he would not come when he was called. We decided that we would use the fast one-word reprimand method to teach him this exercise. We also used the reprimand chain, throwing the check chain near him and reprimanding him until eventually he responded, and came to us.

This might seem a strange response, after we had been reprimanding him!—but what we did was to make him uncomfortable whenever he ran away by making him hear the sound of the chain, and then patting and praising him whenever he came to us.

We worked with Chowsie for half an hour, and by the lesson's end he was coming when called in an enclosed area—we were using a quarter-acre (1 000 square meters) fenced yard. We decided to call a halt to the training for the day.

That night was our first rehearsal for the play with Chowsie. We put him on lead and drove to the rehearsal hall. Unbeknown to us, however, one of our assistants had loosened the little dog's collar. As we alighted from the car, Chowsie slipped out of the collar and ran off down the street, heading for a busy road.

We panicked and began to run after him, yelling his newly given name, which meant absolutely nothing to him. Then we both yelled, "Bah!" The little dog stopped in his tracks, spun around and ran back to us.

When Chowsie completed his first rehearsal that night to everyone's satisfaction, there were no two happier people watching than ourselves. He went on to complete 14 performances in the play, which was a huge success.

By training Chowsie to come when called using a very fast method, we most certainly saved his life. (We would normally have followed all of .the steps outlined in this book, but time was not on our side with Chowsie's training.) To our way of thinking, his crash course had been incomplete, as we had intended to finish off the conditioning the next day. When we called him from the roadside, he responded because he thought that the chain would soon be thrown near him, as this had happened previously when he had run away from us.

And so we realized that the conditioning had worked. Chowsie had responded to that one-word reprimand, despite the fact that, prior to that day, he had never responded to any command at all.

As Chowsie's story tells us, if your dog has been conditioned to the one-word reprimand, it will be easy to teach it to come when called. And, when you want to teach it to come to you while it is off the lead, the results will be both fast and effective.

You should also leave the check chain on your dog, and detach only the training lead. Attach, instead, a very short version of the lightweight cord that you used for teaching your dog to come when called. This shortened cord can be used as a safety net, so to speak, in case you need to gain control of your dog quickly.

Start off with your dog sitting by your side. Step off on your left foot, and say "Walk" in your normal speaking voice. If your dog just sits there or lags behind, then, with your body still facing forward, crouch down, and encourage the dog to follow. Most dogs will approach you faster if you decrease your height.

Never reprimand a dog for lagging either verbally or by checking it. If you do, you will only make it drop back further. Start patting your leg instead—this gesture is seen by a dog as encouragement. Praise it as soon as it comes up beside you. Say "Good dog" in a very pleasant voice, using a high-pitched tone.

There is no need to pat your dog while praising it. You want the dog to get used to being voice-praised, as you are preparing it for those times when it will be working off-lead at a distance from you. If you had to run up to it and pat it at this time, it would mean both a big distraction for your dog and unnecessary exertion for you.

Once you have your dog walking well at your side and in the correct position, voice-praise it and keep walking. If the dog races ahead, passes you or deviates to the side, growl your reprimand word, and then praise it the instant it responds.

Be sure that, when you are walking in one or another direction, you move in a straight line. Do not just amble about—if you do, your dog may bump into you while it is walking.

Now introduce some turns to your pattern—say, a right turn, followed by a left turn, followed by a right about-turn, and a left about-turn. On all left turns and left-about turns, lift your right knee as you turn, gently guiding your dog out of the way. Do this until the dog gets used to these turns.

Continue with these new walking patterns for about 10 minutes, using your one-word

If your dog pulls on the lead, you are using the wrong equipment or holding the lead too tight. Use a check chain or head halter and a 6 ft (2 m) long soft webbing lead. Reprimand and check correctly, and the dog will soon stop pulling.

The reprimand chain is a 3 ft (1 m) length of round-edged link chain. It is thrown near the dog's back legs while giving the reprimand word. Use it to gain control when your dog is distracted or sniffing and ignores the reprimand word.

The only kind way to check a dog: Anchor the lead in your right hand, leave a loop between you, and gather up the slack with your left. Snap and release, then hold the lead loosely again. Check in a straight line past your left thigh.

Teaching your dog to walk correctly: Use the check chain or a quick "Bah!" or "Bad!" when it rushes ahead or sniffs the ground. To check, snap the lead quickly. Do not tug. Praise gently when the dog's shoulder is in line with your legs.

Attentiveness training: Firmly attach a long, lightweight cord (with snap lock and handle) to your dog's lead. Walk in a straight line away from the dog, not speaking to it. When it comes in your direction, turn promptly and go the other way. Repeat.

Making a start with working off-lead: Lay the lead over the dog's back. Use the reprimand word when needed. If the dog becomes distracted or rushes ahead, retrieve the lead to regain control.

First steps to controlling your dog off-lead: Have someone the dog likes take it a short way off. Throw the reprimand chain and use the reprimand word, then crouch with open arms to welcome the dog. Praise it the moment it reaches you.

Ensure you incorporate distractions into the dog's training. Have a friend and the friend's dog walk around you and your dog, or move away from you, with your dog first on then off the lead. Voice reprimand if your dog gets too agitated and wants to move.

The "Recall" off-lead: Let your dog wander a little way off, then throw the reprimand chain to land very near its back legs. Growl your reprimand. As soon as it heads toward you, crouch and speak invitingly. Keep low to appear less dominating.

The "Finish".
Step 1: With your dog sitting in front of you, say "Finish", and take a step backward, pulling the lead past your right thigh as you do.

Step 2: As the dog moves past your right thigh, swap the lead from your right to your left hand.

Step 3: Now step forward on your left foot as you bring your dog around to your left side, placing it gently in the "sit" position. Praise it for a job well done.

reprimand each time your dog steps out of position or makes a mistake. Voice-praise it as soon as it corrects itself. During this time, have a friend walk alongside and try to distract the dog in a pleasant way, by crouching down and encouraging the dog, saying, "Nice dog, good boy," in a high-pitched voice. This will be sufficient distraction for it at this stage. Rapid movements could unsettle or upset it, making it feel threatened.

These initial distractions are important, as you need your dog to be able to concentrate on you no matter who is around, and no matter what other people are doing. Many people tell us that their dogs are very co-operative at home, but as soon as they are taken out they refuse to do anything. This is because these dogs' owners have not incorporated distractions into their training.

After a couple of sessions with your friend distracting your dog, try to arrange to have a session with another person who has a friendly dog you can use as a distraction (see page 63). This will help to make your dog calm around other dogs, so that it does not bound around trying to approach, play with or attack any dog it sees.

Our technique for training a dog to walk correctly off-lead is based on the principle of getting the dog to use its brain as early as possible in the training process. In this way it will learn more quickly. And so we introduce distractions very early to the novice dog—as many distractions as possible, and as early as possible.

We have had much success with this method. Many untrained dogs that would not do anything they were told were reconditioned using the one-word reprimand. Then they were introduced to distractions, and in this way learnt to concentrate from the outset. Within a few minutes all were sitting and staying as required.

The off-lead "recall"

The dog's popularity as a pet is increasing constantly. So, too, is controversy about which aspects of dog behavior are acceptable to the general public, and which are not. More and more restrictions are being placed on dog owners, and more and more fines are being imposed on them by the authorities for the bad behavior of their unruly charges. All of these factors are reinforcing this important message: as dog owners, we have to behave responsibly if we want to continue enjoying the pleasure of these creatures' company.

As modern-day living and its constant pressures make ever greater demands, dog owners are finding that they have less and less time to spend on training and exercising their dogs. When they do manage to get out with their undisciplined dogs, their destination will most often be a public place such as a recreation park or a playing field.

When the untrained dog is unleashed for a run, the trouble starts. If it tries to attack another dog or a child, its owner has very little chance of stopping it from viciously mauling its victim.

If we want to continue to enjoy our dogs and to permit them some freedom, then it is vital that we should be able to call them back to our side at any time. It is also vital that they respond immediately, regardless of what is happening around them.

Training your dog to respond immediately

If you want to train your dog to come back to you as soon as you call it, whether it is on or off the lead, there is a very important principle to follow. It is this: Do not just keep repeating your command to your dog over and over. Give the command, but then follow it quickly with the one-word reprimand: "Rover, come, Bah, Rover come, Bah," not "Rover, come, Rover, come, Rover, come … ." If you always reprimand immediately after the command, your dog will learn to respond immediately, rather than waiting until it feels like it. If you are consistent at this stage, this will pay dividends later, when you may be in a situation where you require your dog to obey you instantly.

To start training your dog for the off-lead "recall," you will need, first of all, a large enclosed area. It is important that your dog cannot escape! Attach your shortened light-weight cord to the dog's check chain, and allow the dog to wander off and investigate. Wait a few minutes and then say its name, followed by "Come."

If your dog responds immediately, praise it lavishly. If it refuses to come immediately, growl "Bah!" or "Bad!" Then, if it still refuses to respond, throw the reprimand chain as close to it as possible. If there is a tree near the dog, throw the chain so that it hits the tree before falling.

Keep throwing the chain and reprimanding; each time, pick up the chain and throw it back, and do this several times until the dog responds. Remember, you have the lightweight cord as a backup if your dog pays no attention at all to you.

Whenever the dog heads toward you, crouch low and speak invitingly to it (see page 63). The lower you are, the less dominating you will seem to your dog, and the more likely it will be to come.

Repeat this exercise several times, making sure you are consistent: each time you do it, reprimand immediately after a command, and praise your dog as soon as it responds correctly.

Teaching the "recall" from the "sit stay"

Place your dog in a "sit", and step away from it, keeping your eye on it as you walk approximately 10 feet (3 m) away. Then stop and face the dog. Wait 10 seconds, and then call it: "Rover, come," raising your hands as you do. This will become the signal later on for your dog to come to you.

If your dog starts approaching once you have called it, slowly crouch down and encourage it to come to you by patting your legs. If your dog has a tendency to overshoot you because of its speedy reaction to being recalled, stand against a wall. It will not be able to shoot past you, and therefore will become accustomed to stopping when it reaches you.

Praise your dog lavishly when it arrives at your side, and pat it into the "sit". In other words, as you are patting your dog, gently place it in the "sit" position, but do not say "Sit." The "sit" should be a position your dog will adopt automatically when it comes to you. It does not need to be commanded to do so.

If you repeat these steps often enough, your dog will soon learn to sit when it comes to you.

Remember, while you are teaching it to do so, never push it or grab it by the muzzle or the scruff. As we have said earlier in this book, your hands must only be associated with gentleness and praise.

The dog that just sits there

If you have a dog that just sits and looks at you when you call it, this is because it is unsure about whether or not it should move from the "stay". Do not be harsh on this type of dog— it is not being stubborn. Some dogs may become confused and think that they should not move once they are in this position. Attach your shortened lightweight lead and gently check your dog toward you (tug it in your direction, tightening and then loosening the lead in

quick succession) as you say "Come," to encourage it to move off the spot. Then run backward, encouraging it as you do. Praise the dog as soon as it responds by moving toward you, and praise it again when it reaches you.

Preventing your dog from anticipating your call

It is wise to vary your methods for calling your dog from the "stay," as some dogs may anticipate the owner's call, and move as soon as they recognize the sound of their own names. The best way to prevent this from happening is by sometimes calling out the dog's name, followed quickly by "Stay," and then, at other times, calling the dog's name, followed quickly by "Come."

With this method, the dog will not know what is coming next, and will learn to wait for the command before responding.

Teaching your dog the "finish" command

The straight-to-the-finish "recall"

In some parts of the world, dog owners prefer to have their dogs go straight to their left side rather than coming and sitting in front first. To the owners' way of thinking, they need their dogs to be ready to walk off with them immediately. They do have a point, but some countries' trials regulations state that the dog must first come and sit in front, and then go to the "heel" position. Either way, this is known as the "finish."

You can teach your dog to do what you want it to, or whatever trial regulations require. If you want the dog to go straight to your left side as it comes to you in the "recall," simply put your right hand down to pat it. At the same time, let your left hand guide its rump, swinging the dog around to sit on your left side in the desired position— facing forward, as you will be.

Using another technique, you can get your dog to go straight around your right side. Attach the small lightweight cord; as your dog approaches in the "recall", gently take hold of the cord and step backward. Then take one step forward as you guide your dog around to your left side, and swap the cord from your right hand to your left hand as you are guiding it into the "sit" position on this side (see page 64).

For both of these techniques, there is no need to give any command other than the "Come" command, as the whole exercise should be completed by the dog on the one command.

"Finish" as a separate command

In the first two techniques for teaching the "finish," the two actions of "recalling" and "finishing" are part of a single sequence. With the third technique for teaching the "finish," however, the two actions are treated as separate entities. The dog will have finished its "recall" and will be sitting in front of you waiting for your next command. Now you will get it to do the "finish."

At most training schools, owners are taught that, when they wish their dogs to take up the "finish" position on their left side after entering from the right side and circling around the back of their legs, they should command the dog to "Heel." However, we feel that this is very confusing for the dog, because, to a dog, the "Heel" command generally means that it must move off by your side and keep walking beside you until told otherwise.

Faster results can be achieved by using the command "Finish"—for no other reason than that the dog will not get confused.

If a different command is used from the one for getting it to walk at heel, the dog will learn the exercise much more quickly, and it will not be in any doubt about what you want it to do.

To teach the "Finish" command, attach your light-weight cord to your dog's check chain before doing the "recall" from the "sit." Then, when your dog has come to you after being called, pat it gently, and at the same time take hold of the lead with your right hand. Command "Finish" as you take one step back and then one step forward, swapping the cord to your left hand and bringing the dog around to your left side. Praise it, and make it sit as you are doing so. See the pictures on page 64 for further reference.

Chapter Five

Advanced training

In this chapter, we will first explain how to teach your dog each of the advanced exercises, and then describe the benefits of the exercise. The variety of training exercises presented here will help you and your dog to develop a greater understanding of each other, and become closer companions.

Advanced training is where the fun begins for you and your dog. This is not to say that basic training is not enjoyable—for both of you. However, when your dog starts learning the more advanced exercises, you will see a new spring in its step.

This form of training allows your dog more freedom than basic training, but still teaches it something that will benefit both of you. Your dog will love learning exercises that require neither the restraints of the lead nor the tedious repetition of tasks.

Teaching your dog to jump

Before you can teach your dog how to jump over obstacles, there are a few things you will have to do. The first will be to ensure that your dog is physically fit, and that it does not have any major hip or shoulder problems. It may be necessary for you to get your veterinarian to give the dog a medical checkup before you start teaching it this exercise.

You must also be certain that your dog is fully grown before you teach it to jump. Most breeds reach this stage of development by around 12 months of age, but some of the larger breeds, such as the Great Danes and Newfoundlands, are only fully grown after about two years. If in doubt, check with the breeder.

The more varied the objects you choose for your dog to jump over the better. Then it will not end up believing it is only allowed to jump over a specific type of obstacle.

Our dog Monty's actions (see opposite), show clearly that he was not a dog who jumped whenever he felt like it—this, too, could become an awkward situation. He jumped over the wall only when commanded. (Note that it is not wise to teach your dog to jump over its own fence! It is a better idea to use a constructed jump, a log, etc.)

THE WALL IS NO MATCH FOR OUR MONTY

During the time we were teaching our German shepherd, Monty, to 'leap tall buildings', Sylvia visited with a friend who worked at a nearby office building. When she arrived with Monty, our friend's young child was also there. This mischievous little boy was in the habit of locking every gate or door in sight, and when Sylvia and her friend weren't looking, he closed the self-locking door in the office courtyard on poor Monty. And the office security guard was the only one who had a key!

Sylvia and the boy's mother couldn't lift Monty out and our friend became concerned that she might lose her job if the security guard had to be called. Then Sylvia had an idea. What about commanding Monty to jump over the wall? Even though it was over 6 feet (2 m) high, he had scaled walls higher than this at the German Shepherd Dog Club without much difficulty.

She called out, "Over!"

Monty just looked at the wall and barked back as if to say: "Are you serious?"

Sylvia smiled. "Bah," she said, and then again, "Over."

Now Monty was starting to eye the wall. It was clear he was thinking, "She is serious."

He crouched, and sprang at the wall.

"Good boy," Sylvia assured him.

Then he clambered and scratched his way to the top of the wall, grabbing with his front paws and pulling himself up. Sylvia encouraged him to leap to the ground, and then broke his fall with her arm as he did so. He was very happy to be free again!

Although Monty's adventure was not a life-threatening situation, his jumping training certainly saved the day.

The method

When introducing your dog to jumping for the first time, you will need to have a solid obstacle for it to jump over, so that it cannot go under the object instead of getting over it.

Then place your dog on a 3-ft (1-m) lead, and step over the obstacle. Command the dog: "Over." It is important that you actually step over the jump yourself and do not walk around, as your dog will try to imitate you. Keep the lead short and place your dog close to the obstacle, so that it cannot attempt to go around it instead. Each time the dog completes the exercise correctly and jumps over the obstacle, praise it lavishly, and then step over the obstacle again yourself (see page 81).

Gradually increase the height of the jump over a period of a few days, being sure that you do not exceed the recommended level for your particular breed. The heights for specific breeds are available through the canine association in your area.

The rule of thumb generally is that a dog should be able to jump its own height at the shoulder—this rule applies even to the larger breeds, such as the Great Dane and the Newfoundland.

Teaching your dog to bark on command

Many complaints are heard nowadays about noisy dogs that nuisance bark. Many local councils have huge penalties for the owners of noisy dogs.

However, there are times when you may want your dog to bark—as a trick to show your friends, or when a threatening stranger enters your property, or even for television or movie work. Some movie makers require a dog that will bark reliably whenever required for a particular scene. And the only way to predict that a dog will bark when required is to train it to bark on command.

If you train your dog to bark, this does not mean that it will become a nuisance barker. As mentioned earlier, dogs learn by association, and so a trained dog will normally bark only in situations it has learnt to associate with the need to bark, rather than just barking all the time. If, after you have trained your dog to bark, it does bark excessively, reprimand it each time it barks without first being commanded to do so.

Most dogs will bark at some time in their lives, and some dogs are more vocal than others. There are certain breeds, too, that bark more than others. Some of the more yappy breeds are the collie, the Australian cattle dog, the Chihuahua, the various terriers, and the sheepdogs.

Of course, if you own a basenji, it won't bark, but it may howl. Basenjis don't bark at all, and nor do some of the wild dog species, because barking in the wild would betray the dog's presence and position to prey and to other hunters like itself.

The method

To teach your dog to bark on command, you will need to start by finding something that usually makes it bark. Alternatively, you could try holding some food up and exciting the dog with your voice. Or you could tie the dog up and remain a little way off while running around or bouncing a ball. If you have no success with any of these, try anything else that could possibly get your dog to bark!

As soon as the dog starts barking, or even whimpering— that is, each time your dog utters a sound—say "Bark," or "Speak." Practice regularly, and keep saying the word every time the dog barks. Eventually it will respond by barking when it hears the command word.

Some dogs will take longer to learn this than others. Puppies usually catch on very quickly, and are easy to excite and get barking. In general, you should be able to teach your dog to bark on command in anywhere from four to 12 weeks, provided that you are training it regularly each day.

Teaching your dog to fetch (retrieve)

Fetching is a natural thing for most dogs to do, especially those that were bred specifically for this purpose. The retrieval breeds are the Labrador, the golden retriever and the curly-coated retriever, to name only a few. These types of dogs will pick up anything in their mouths and carry it around without too much persistence on your part, but it will take a little longer for you to teach them to come and sit in front of you and hold the object until you remove it from their mouths.

There are several breeds that are not natural retrievers: the Doberman, the German shepherd, the Rottweiler, the collie, and some of the smaller lapdog types, again to name only a few. However, all dogs can be trained to fetch and carry something—but doing so must be fun for them.

Teaching a natural fetcher

If your dog is a natural retriever but lacks the finishing touches required for entering a competition, or if you just want more control over it, then follow the instructions in this section to get your dog to fetch an object, deliver the object to you and hold it in its mouth until you command: "Give!"

What normally happens with dogs is, as soon as you try to introduce anything remotely regimental, they lose interest. So what you will have to do initially is to separate the two actions of retrieving and holding the object. Play the "throw the object" game, allowing your dog to chase an object and bring it to you and maybe even drop it at your feet. The aim of the game is to get the dog to deliver to you an object it has fetched.

Then teach your dog to hold the object. Start off with a soft item that will not hurt its mouth, such as a rolled-up piece of vinyl or a length of rolled towelling. Ensure that the object is not too large—it should fit into the dog's mouth with ease.

Place your dog on-lead, and stand on the lead so that it cannot run away. Gently open its mouth, and say "Hold." We use the command "Hold" here because, once you put the two exercises—fetching and holding—together, you will be able to ask your dog to keep holding the object rather than dropping it once it has retrieved it for you.

Place the object in the dog's mouth, just behind its fangs, and tilt its head back slightly so that it cannot spit the object out. Reprimand with your one-word reprimand word at the precise moment your dog tries to eject the object, and praise as soon as it stops trying to do so.

Initially, just getting your dog to hold the object while you are tilting its head back is sufficient. Leave the object in for only five seconds, making a big fuss of your dog as soon as you take the object gently out of its mouth.

Once you have your dog holding an object successfully and happily, go back to throwing the object, asking the dog to "Hold" as it comes closer to you, and praising as it does so.

Use only a very soft tone when reprimanding in this exercise—you want your dog to enjoy it.

Eventually, the fetching and holding actions will become a single exercise for your dog, and you will be able to phase out the "Hold" command. Then, to get your dog to adopt the "sit" position with the object in its mouth, just pat it gently, and, as you are doing so, press gently down on its rump until it sits. With both patience and practice, the command "Fetch" will eventually cause your dog to run out and grab an object (see page 81), bring it back to you, and then sit in front of you and hold the object until you command "Give."

Even though your dog may already be happy to carry sticks and other large objects for you, you will need to follow these guidelines when training it to fetch for you.

Remember that the purpose of this exercise is to harness your dog's chasing and fetching action so that you will be able to predict what it will do. Otherwise it will fetch objects only when it feels like it, and will not be a reliable retriever.

Remember, too, that you still want your dog to have fun chasing objects that you throw for it, and training it to "fetch" means teaching it a regimented exercise that, to the dog's way of thinking, will not be fun at first.

So, the more pleasant you can make the process, the faster the dog will accept it.

Teaching a dog that runs away with the object

If your dog is the type that runs to get the object thrown, and then runs away with it, you will need to use the one-word reprimand. If it then responds by coming to you, praise it. If it drops the object, throw it again.

If the dog still keeps running away, do not chase it. Instead, select an area where your dog has to come to you and cannot avoid you—such an area should have only one way out, and should preferably be narrow. For example, you may choose a passageway or an area at the side of your house that is blocked off by a fence.

Once your dog is unable to run away from you because of the confined area in which you are training it, it will have to run to you. As it attempts to run past you, block its path, and then praise it lavishly, acting as if it has done the most wonderful thing imaginable.

The first time you do the training, repeat this process several times. Then do the same thing each evening for the next few days. This will lead the dog to realize that the reward is better when it brings the object to you than when it escapes. (You could also try giving your dog a treat, when it gives you the object despite its obvious reluctance to relinquish its find!)

The benefits of getting your dog to fetch things for you do not need to be explained—and you will find it even more useful to have a dog that is willing to give up what it has fetched without a struggle!

Teaching your dog to find

Someone once said to us that a dog's sense of smell, compared to a human's, was like the difference between an envelope and a stamp—the human's olfactory sense being the stamp. Humans have about five million olfactory cells, and a German shepherd has two hundred million. (The number does differ from breed to breed; some breeds may have fewer olfactory cells than others.)

The dog relies heavily on its scenting powers and, of all of its senses, smell gets the final say. For example, if you placed a

MONTY FINDS THE MONEY

We can vividly remember the day our daughter Donna, then only four years old, asked if she could go and buy an ice cream from the van that regularly came to our street on the weekends.

We gave her the last coin we had on us at the time, and she ran off happily to buy a cone. In no time she was back, crying. The coin had been flung out of her hand as she ran to the van, and was lost in the long grass at the side of the road.

We tried looking, but to no avail—it was a small coin, and the area was vast. We decided to give our dog Monty a go at finding the money, but did not hold out much hope because of the smallness of the object. We allowed him to sniff Donna's arm, and then commanded, "Seek."He bounded away, sniffing the ground as he went.

We watched as he circled around, pushing his nose deep into the lush grass. Then suddenly he appeared to have given up. He returned to us, wagging his tail.

"Never mind, feller, " we said. "You tried your best." He nuzzled his nose against our legs, and then spat out a small coin.

Donna was delighted, and ran to catch the ice-cream van before it moved off. Monty was given a nice big juicy bone for his wonderful efforts.

This was not the last time that, thanks to Monty, we found things we had thought were lost forever!

stuffed tiger in your living room, your dog would most likely bristle, growl or bark at first sighting. Its eyes would be relaying a message to its brain that this was a real threat. However, once it was able to sniff the tiger, it would soon realize that this creature was not alive, and a further message would be relayed to the effect that it posed no threat. Once this new message was received in the brain, the dog would probably ignore the tiger altogether.

The method

This is an invaluable exercise to teach your dog. You will probably use it regularly for finding articles you have lost such as dropped keys, wallets or even money.

To teach your dog how to find objects as Monty was taught, you will need a small wallet or glove that has your scent on it, a screw-top jar with diced meat or a special treat for the dog—preferably a food type that is not too soft, and therefore easy to handle.

Place your dog in a "sit", and walk out in a direct line in front of it until you are approximately 25 paces away. Then, opening the jar, take some food out of it and place it on the ground.

Return to your dog, and command "Seek" over and over, gently leading it toward the spot where you left the food. Allow it to eat the food, praising it as it does. Repeat this process several times, each time extending the distance until eventually you are moving out of sight—say, behind a tree or a hedge—taking the food with you. If you go out of the dog's sight temporarily, you will be getting the dog to start using its nose: if it cannot see where you placed the food, it will have to start sniffing the ground to find it.

Once your dog has found the hidden food several times, start from the beginning again, placing the food close to your dog and then gradually moving it out of sight. But now you should be placing the wallet or glove you have with you next to the food, and getting your dog to pick it up immediately after it eats the food each time.

Praise your dog lavishly as it picks up the item, and then run backward toward where you first placed it in the "sit". Now get the dog to bring the item to you. It is not absolutely necessary to go all the way to the exact spot, as long as your dog does get accustomed to bringing the item to you over some distance.

Continue this until your dog is finding the food and bringing the object of its own volition.

Jumping: Keep your dog on lead very close to the obstacle so it cannot walk around it. Then step over the obstacle yourself. Next, encourage the dog to copy you, saying "Over" as you direct it over the jump with the lead.

Fetching: Keep the training fun, and your dog will fetch anything you throw. If you want to train it for competition work, it should be able to fetch a dumbbell on command.

Tracking: While a friend holds your dog on a long lead, walk a short way off and hide. Now the friend should let the dog look for you, saying "Track, track" as it seeks. Praise the dog lavishly when it finds you.

Scent discrimination the easy way.
Step 1: Put several pairs of clean or new socks on the ground along with a pair you have recently worn. If your dog sniffs at or picks up the wrong socks, don't react.

Step 2: Once the dog picks up the right pair of socks, praise it, crouching as it brings the socks to you. Later, also use wooden, metal and leather objects.

Dropping at a distance: Use a voice command and a clear hand signal, preferably away from your body. Reprimand if the dog keeps running. If necessary, step toward it and place it on the spot where it should have dropped.

Bowing: Start with your dog on your left and put your left hand gently under its belly as you press softly with your right hand on its shoulders, saying "Bow". Praise it as it does so.

Weaving: Pass your dog's favorite toy or ball between your legs and say "Through." As you move the ball away through your own legs, it will follow. Now repeat in the opposite direction.

Jumping through a hoop: Start by holding the hoop close to the ground, and your dog's favorite ball or toy on the opposite side, so that the dog has to jump through to get to it. Say "Through" as the dog jumps, and praise it.

83

Carrying objects: Teach your dog to carry things for you by introducing it to small, light objects first.

Catching a Frisbee: This is a fun game for you and your dog. Begin by throwing morsels of food for it to catch.

Dogs love the flyball machine, but it takes a bit of practice. The dog pushes down the pedal, flinging the tennis ball into the air, and then jumps to catch it.

Once this happens, repeat the exercise again, but this time without leaving any food next to the object. Follow your dog to the spot, and as soon as it starts to look for the food, command "Seek," and make sure that the dog picks up the article.

Again, praise it and then run backward. This time reward your dog with the food on its return to you. Be sure to leave the unused food in the sealed jar; otherwise your dog will lose concentration as it looks for its treat. Keep control with your one-word reprimand if the dog starts sniffing around.

Praise your dog for bringing the article to you, take the object, and then feed the dog immediately. Repeat this about five times more, and then discontinue using the food altogether.

Then repeat this exercise over the next few days, again phasing out the food as soon as you feel your dog is enthusiastically seeking out the object.

Be sure not to tire your dog by doing too many "seeks"— about four a day are sufficient after your introductory training session. Your dog will become uninterested if the exercise starts to become tedious. After a few days, change the pattern by taking the dog with you, making it walk correctly by your side and dropping your article behind you while you are walking.

Make sure your dog does not see you drop the object, as you need to be sure that it will use its nose to find the object. (If you do not do this, then, when you really lose something, your dog will not be able to find it, as it may be accustomed to finding objects only when it has seen you dropping them.)

You will need to cover a reasonable distance, and your path should follow a horseshoe shape; start at one end of the horseshoe and finish at the other. Once you reach the end, about-turn, and send your dog back in the direction from which you have just come from, commanding "Seek."

Continue this exercise until your dog is confidently seeking out article you have dropped each time you practice. Change articles from time to time so that the dog becomes accustomed to finding all types of objects for you, and change the pattern you walk in also.

Teaching your dog to track

When teaching your dog to track you or to find someone, you will again be requiring the dog to use its nose.

A dog relies heavily on its sense of smell. It has an innate ability to decipher scents and follow a particular scent.

However, some dogs are better than others at tracking. The best trackers are the hunting breeds—the pointer, the retriever, the spaniel, and those breeds that have long muzzles, such as the German shepherd, the Doberman and the Australian cattle dog.

Breeds with shorter muzzles, such as the boxer, the bulldog and the pug, to name only a few, have a lower success rate in tracking their quarry than dogs with longer muzzles. However, these breeds still make very competent trackers.

The method

Most dogs love sniffing, so it's relatively easy to teach your dog to track.

Have on hand a screw top jar with some diced food or meat to give as a treat to your dog when it finds you. You will need a firm fitting leather collar or a tracking harness (available from your local pet shop) and a 20-ft (6-m) long soft webbing lead or a horse lunging lead.

Have a friend accompany you to a large field or park and have your assistant hold your dog as you walk a short distance and hide (see page 81). Your assistant should then let your dog lead him or her to where you are hiding. The dog should run to the spot where you stood before you hid, then put its nose to the ground and follow your scent to your hiding place. Praise your dog and give it a treat.

Repeat several times over the next few weeks, increasing the distance and varying the time that your assistant waits before allowing your dog to find you. Once your dog is proficient at finding you, you could have your friend hide next, then use other people and even strangers to the dog.

Never let the dog run free to track. This exercise must always be carried out on-lead in case the dog runs off and gets lost.

CASEY FINDS THE CLUE

A somewhat serious situation was averted by the tracking ability of a lovable mutt called Casey. She was a crossbred bearded collie-standard poodle who belonged to Simon, a friend of ours, and she was a wonderful tracking dog.

A three-year-old named Sara once became lost in the wild in Simon's district. A search was launched, and when Simon heard about it he decided to see if Casey might be able to help find the little girl.

He had Sara's mother fetch her daughter's pajamas that had been worn the night before. Simon held the garments to Casey's nose, and immediately she began to whine.

"Track," Simon said, and she calmly put her nose to the ground and began sniffing it, circling and doubling back until she appeared to pick up on a scent. She carried on like this for about an hour until eventually she led Simon to what appeared to be an old mine site. She now appeared to be very excited, and began whining.Suddenly she stopped at the mouth of a mine shaft. She began to wag her tail and bark excitedly as she peered into the shaft.

Simon knelt down beside Casey and looked into the darkened shaft. As his eyes became accustomed to the dark, he could see a frail little figure huddled against a wall.

It was Sara. She just sat there, staring into his eyes. Simon told her that her parents would be with her soon, and ran back to find the search party and tell them where she had fallen. He later found out that the family had searched around the same area earlier and had called her name, but the child had failed to answer them.

Soon Sara and her family were reunited, and the little girl made a full recovery from her trauma.

Casey was called upon many times after that day to assist the police in the area, until they finally obtained their own tracking dogs.

Teaching your dog to distinguish scents

Getting a dog to distinguish scents is probably one of the most difficult training exercises. Dogs normally do this as a matter of course, but on an instinctive level only. It will be difficult to pass on to the dog what you require it to do, because the action you want it to learn is not a visible one that you can demonstrate.

For example, if you give a reprimand when a dog picks up the wrong article instead of the one you wanted it to, this could easily be misconstrued by the dog: it may think that it should not pick up any article at all. You will therefore have to be very careful indeed with this exercise.

Follow these steps, and you will be able to communicate quickly to your dog exactly what you want it to do—without causing any confusion.

The method

Find a pair of socks that you have worn recently, and roll them into a ball. Don't be concerned about the fact that they have been on your feet—your dog will love them!

Sit your dog beside you, and throw the socks on the ground about 6 feet (2 m) away. Tell the dog to "Find," or give any other relevant command you feel comfortable with; whatever you choose, keep it brief.

If your dog is reliable about fetching objects, it should have no hesitation about picking up the socks and bringing them straight to you (see page 82). If it refuses, to pick up the socks, pick them up and throw them a bit further away, or attempt to excite the dog by shaking them and then throwing them on the ground again, commanding "Find," or using another command you have chosen.

Once your dog is freely picking the socks up and bringing them back, place some clean or new socks on the ground, and now put the dirty socks in the middle of the pile.

Then send the dog in again, commanding "Find," and praising it as soon as it sniffs at the right pair of socks. Don't say anything if it sniffs the wrong one. If you reprimand the dog while it is sniffing and searching, this could put it off the exercise altogether.

Some exuberant breeds will just dash out and grab the first thing they see. If your dog brings back the wrong socks, do not reprimand it. Just remove the pair it has brought you and try again, only praising the dog when it picks up the right pair of socks.

The idea behind using the socks is to remove all doubts from the dog's mind as to what the exercise is all about. The strong smell from the dirty socks will help your dog to learn your objective very quickly!

Once your dog is regularly doing this exercise correctly, use some pieces of wood instead of socks.

Keep one piece of wood for your own personal use, and place it either in your belt close to your skin or in another position such as up your sleeve, in order to make sure it has a lot of your scent on it. Once it has been there for a while, throw your "scented" piece of wood onto the ground and have your dog fetch it.

Repeat the exercise a few times before placing another unscented piece of wood on the ground in front of the dog. Then add another unscented piece, and later yet another. Use tongs to place the unscented sticks on the ground. Only add each subsequent piece of wood once your dog gets the right piece of wood—the scented one—each time. Initially it is preferable that no one else apart from you touches the wood—both the scented and the unscented pieces—but later on, once your dog is doing the exercise correctly, this will not matter.

Keep adding pieces of wood until you have about six pieces on the ground, and your dog is selecting the right piece each time it does the exercise.

Repeat this exercise regularly over the next few days. Vary the types of objects you use—for example, you may use some pieces of leather, or some small pieces of metal pipe.

Teaching your dog to drop at a distance

As we have shown earlier in this book, getting your dog to drop when it is far away is a very useful technique. You may even save its life! (See "Monty Avoids Misfortune" in Chapter Two.)

To get your dog to drop at a distance, you will first need to accustom it to dropping on the exact spot it has reached as you are giving the command. Because it will be used to dropping at your side, having learnt the "drop" in this position, when commanded to drop it will more than likely try to walk toward you: it will associate the "drop" with being close to you.

To help your dog make the transition easily from the drop beside you to the drop at a distance, start off by standing close to it, and having it facing you in a standing position and on lead. You can allow it to walk around if you want to.

You will need to use the command "Drop," and give a hand signal as you do. Your signal may be one of your own choice, but it will need to include a slight movement of your right hand away from your body, then a slight movement upward, and then another down again, pointing at the ground (see page 82). Reprimand with your one-word reprimand if your dog fails to respond and just keeps walking.

As you signal with your right hand, step forward immediately and gently push your dog into a "drop" with your left hand, praising it as you do. Then step back to where you started from. Allow 10 seconds to pass, and then say "Free," and encourage your dog to move.

Repeat the "dropping at a distance" exercise several times. Then extend the distance until your dog is dropping anything up to about 50 feet (15 m) away. If the dog refuses to respond to your command and drop immediately, move rapidly toward it to place it in the "drop." Be careful not to frighten it.

Once the dog realizes what you want, it will stop moving, and will eventually adopt the "drop" position every time you say "Drop."

Chapter 6

Teaching your dog tricks

If you really want to have some fun with your dog, this chapter is for you. All dogs love doing tricks, and learning them will be a welcome break from the more regimented obedience exercises. You will, however, need to have some control over your dog in order to teach it most of these tricks.

In this chapter, as you will see, we mostly use three things to help us get the desired results quickly. These are a tennis ball, food and praise—the things that dogs love. Decide whether it is some food or a tennis ball that is most likely to excite your dog enough to get it to perform the trick required. Praise should be used in every exercise, as this is the only way your dog will know that it is doing what you require.

In all of the following exercises, be sure not to overwork your dog. Most dogs will only perform an exercise happily four or five times in a row; then it becomes work. Keep this in mind if you want your dog to enjoy its training.

Sitting up

This trick is relatively easy for smaller dogs, and some dogs will adopt this position with little coercion. However, most long-bodied breeds, such as the dachshund, will probably not be able to master the trick. With dogs such as these, you should perhaps concentrate on other tricks instead.

Some of the larger breeds will find sitting up a bit more difficult to master. However, there is no reason they should not be able to do this trick— with patience on your part.

Select a non-slip area, and have your dog sit there. Then lift both of its front paws over your arm and attempt to balance its body fully over its hindquarters, saying "Beg" as you do so. Try to get your dog to balance by itself without using your arm as a brace, even if only for a few seconds, and as soon as it does so, praise the dog and allow it to return to its original position.

Repeat this three or four times over the next few days, or until your dog performs the "sit up" without assistance.

Food could be used to entice your dog to perform this trick. Simply hold the food above its head once it is in the "sit," keeping the food just out of its reach. Give it the food as soon as it balances for a few seconds, and then allow it to go free.

Bowing

This is a simple little trick to teach your dog, and a real heart-winner. Place the dog in a stand on lead and gently press on its shoulders with your right hand, saying "Bow" as you gently place your left hand under its belly, preventing it from going into a "drop" (see page 83).

With daily practice, your dog will very quickly learn to do this adorable trick.

Playing dead

How many times have you been moved to tears while watching a "Lassie" movie, or another movie with a doggy hero, where the star has been wounded and is lying on its side looking as if it is at death's door? Well, that dog was only "playing dead."

If your dog is reliable with the correct response to the "drop stay" exercise, it will not take much to teach it this trick. Kneel down beside it and gently grip it under the chin with your right hand. Then, keeping the head firm, roll the dog onto its side.

It does not matter which way you roll your dog. The side you choose should be the one toward which your dog is leaning; for instance, if your dog is lying on its left hip, or leaning to the left, roll it that way. As you start rolling the dog, say "Play dead," and praise it when it has rolled over onto its side. Use your one-word reprimand if it resists you.

Have your dog stay in this position for a minute, and then say "Free," and praise it lavishly.

Repeat this exercise daily so that your dog will do the trick reliably whenever you want it to, including times when other people or dogs are present.

Crawling

Again, this is a fairly simple trick to teach your dog, providing that it is reliable in the "drop" exercises. However, if you have a dog that you intend to trial in competitions, delay training the dog to do this exercise until you have attained all of your titles. The reason for this is that your dog could become confused between the "drop stay" and the "crawl" exercise, and may start to crawl forward instead of "staying" as requested.

To teach your dog how to crawl, place it in a "drop" while on lead and gather the lead up short in your right hand. Keep your left hand on your dog's back to prevent it from standing up. Remember that, in order to crawl, your dog will have to lift its shoulders slightly, so be sure you allow for this.

Gently tug the lead toward you and move forward as you do to encourage forward movement from your dog. Say "Crawl." Praise your dog for any small attempt at forward movement.

This trick will take a lot of practice, and you must ensure that you do not place any weight on your dog's back. Be sure that you balance yourself before starting, by standing with your legs slightly apart. Practice the "crawl" regularly, but no more than four times a day.

Weaving

All types of breeds love this trick, and it is a very easy one to teach your dog.

You will need a tennis ball or your dog's favorite toy, and a 3-ft (1-m) long lead on your dog. Hold the object and the lead in your right hand. Then, with your dog in the normal walking position, and with both of you facing forward, hold your legs apart and pass the lead between them in a straight line, leading the dog through as you do (see page 83). Say "Through."

Let your dog see the ball, but keep the object just out of the dog's reach as you pass it back through your legs on the next step you take. Make the dog pass between your legs as you do.

This exercise should be done slowly at first; otherwise you could find yourself and your dog in one big tangle on the ground!

Again, lots of practice is needed, over a period of a week or so. Take care not to let your dog tire of the exercise.

Jumping through a hoop

Teaching your dog to jump through a hoop is really just an extension of the jumping exercise. The only difference is that your dog will have to jump through the hoop, whereas with the jumping exercise you have taught it to jump over things. Learning to jump through instead of over something will require only a small adjustment on your dog's part.

To teach this trick, you will need either a cane hoop or an old bicycle rim, and your dog's favorite ball or toy. Start off by holding the hoop close to the ground, and the object on the opposite side, so that the dog has to jump through the hoop to get to it. Say "Through" as the dog jumps, and praise it as it completes the exercise.

Again, practice does make perfect. Just keep adjusting the height of the hoop until your dog is jumping comfortably through it every time.

Jumping over the owner's back

This exercise is another variation on the jumping exercise, except that this time your dog will be jumping over your back.

You will need help with this exercise, so ask someone with whom the dog is familiar to help you.

Your dog will need to be on lead. Have your helper hold it while you crouch down on the ground on all fours.

Because your dog may take this exercise as an invitation to play, the reprimand word may be used, but your assistant will have to do any reprimanding necessary, because with your lowered height a reprimand from you will probably be ignored by the dog.

Once you are in position, have your assistant say "Over" as he or she runs toward you with a shortened lead.

At this stage your dog may just jump onto your back, but with a good reprimand from your assistant and a snap of the lead as he or she runs past you, the dog will go where it should.

Have your assistant repeat this exercise several times, each time giving the command "Over" and praising the dog as it jumps over your back.

Once your dog understands the exercise, and with practice, you will eventually be able to place your dog in a "sit," command "Over," and have it go sailing over your back.

You can increase your height by raising yourself slightly, and thereby increase the height your dog jumps. Be sure, however, that the height is not too difficult for your dog to clear.

Carrying objects

When teaching your dog to carry things, you will have to consider the shape and size of the object you want the dog to carry, and also the weight of the object. Also keep your dog's height and size in mind.

The shape of the object is important because an undesirably shaped article may interfere with your dog's movements, bumping the dog as it attempts to carry it. Our dogs carry brooms, buckets, baskets, briefcases, newspapers and telephone directories, to name but a few things, but we had to introduce these items gradually by first teaching them to carry smaller and lighter items, and then building up to the larger items. This way they were able to adjust gradually to the heavier articles.

Start by teaching your dog to hold a rolled newspaper in its mouth, and take two steps back, encouraging the dog to take a few steps toward you. Say "Bring" as you do so. If your dog already fetches things, you won't have much trouble teaching it this exercise. If the dog won't hold the newspaper, however, revert to teaching it to hold a soft item first, as described in Chapter Five, under the heading "Teaching a natural fetcher".

Once you have your dog carrying a newspaper successfully, progress slowly to different items such as small books, soft toys and your dog's own lead (folded, so that it does not entangle the dog's legs as it moves).

If you don't rush these exercises, your dog will learn to enjoy carrying objects for you.

Doing the shopping

This used to be a popular trick. However, we do not think that dogs should be allowed to wander off by themselves. They could be set upon by marauding dogs, or they may be hit by an approaching vehicle while attempting to cross the road.

This is a great trick to teach your dog for television or movie work, as some agencies call for dogs that can perform this trick. Also, some dogs are more focused than others and could learn to do part of the trick without getting into difficulties. Bessie, described in the story below, is a very focused dog who wants only to serve her master. She is a wonderfully intelligent animal; indeed, we feel that she is unique.

Our method for getting your own dog to do the shopping

BESSIE BUYS THE GROCERIES

An old man we know owns a Labrador called Bessie, who does all his shopping for him.

Bessie always used to accompany her owner when he went to the stores, carrying the shopping basket for him to the butcher's and the grocer's, and then back home again.

When her owner became too sick to go out, Bessie, knowing the way blindfolded after years of going with him to do the shopping, pestered him with constant barking. Eventually he gave her a note, the basket and some money, and let her go on her own.

The local butcher and grocer know Bessie by sight, and greet her as she arrives, carrying the basket in her mouth. Each reads the note from her owner, puts the items required in the basket, replaces the note, takes payment and gives the usual "Goodbye." Then Bessie trots off to the next store, heading for home as soon as she has finished her task.

shows you how to get it to take a basket from one person to the next. It does not show you how to get the dog to actually go out on its own, for the reasons we have given above.

Select a well-shaped shopping basket that your dog can hold comfortably, and will not bump against its chest. Put in some lightweight groceries, or some empty packets. You can increase the weight later, once your dog learns to carry the weight of the basket (see page 84).

Teach the dog to carry the basket by putting it in its mouth, waiting a few seconds, and then saying "Give." You will not usually need a command for the first part of the action, while your dog is holding the basket— it will probably understand that you want it to hold something in its mouth because of similar exercises you have already taught it.

Once you are sure that your dog does know how to "hold," walk backward away from it, encouraging it to bring the basket to you, and saying "Bring" as you do so. Eventually, "Bring" will become the dog's command word for this exercise.

Catching a Frisbee

The easiest way to teach your dog to catch a Frisbee is to use the following three steps.

Step 1: Place your dog in a "sit," and, standing about 6 feet (2 m) in front of it, throw small morsels of food to it and say "Catch" as you do so.

Step 2: Once your dog is successfully catching the food morsels, use a tennis ball. With the dog again about 6 feet (2 m) away from you, throw the ball to it so that it can catch it with its mouth. Praise the dog as soon as it catches the ball. Keep practicing over the next few days, making sure you do not practice any exercise more than five times.

Step 3: Once your dog is doing step two easily, introduce the Frisbee. This time, place your dog in a sit about 10 feet (3 m) away. Throw the Frisbee so it moves a little way above your dog's head, saying "Catch" as you do. Repeat this four or five times, trying to finish the session on a good note: with your dog catching the Frisbee (see page 84).

Bringing another dog in on a lead

To get your dog to do this trick, you will firstly need to practice getting your dog to fetch its lead. You will also need to find another dog that is compatible with your own.

Place your dog's lead on the ground. Show it where the lead is, and ask it to "Bring."

Have your dog bring the lead to you a few times, and then attach the lead to an article such as a rolled-up towel or a small blanket. Now have your dog again bring its lead to you, only this time you will need to encourage the dog to drag the extra weight by praising it the instant it appears to feel the extra burden.

Once your dog has mastered this, attach the lead to the friendly dog that is helping you, or have another person hold the lead, and get your dog to bring this person to you.

Again, practicing this exercise will ensure that your dog performs the trick reliably.

Playing with the flyball

The diagram on page 100 will give you an idea of the construction of a flyball machine. Also look at the photograph on page 84. The basic principle is that, if you place a tennis ball in the ball cup, and the dog pushes down the paw pad, or pedal, the mechanical arm will throw the ball. Then, as the ball flies up into the air—hence its name—the dog can do the second part of the trick: catching it.

This is one trick that all dogs love. We well remember the first time we trained our dog to activate the flyball. He sat for ages next to the ball waiting for it to fly into the air, not realizing that if he stepped on the pedal he could make it fly himself. Eventually he did learn how to activate the ball, and it remains his favorite game to this day.

To teach your own dog to activate the flyball, stand astride the dog very close to the pedal. Both of you should be facing the machine. Excite your dog by using your voice, saying "Get your ball." Try to excite the dog enough so that it reaches out with its paw and strikes the pedal of the flyball. When this does happen, praise the dog, and then release it so that it can catch the ball.

If you have a dog that is either slow to learn or hard to excite, you will have to lift its paw and press it on the pedal.

Be sure to practice regularly until your dog can do the trick on its own.

FLYBALL MACHINE

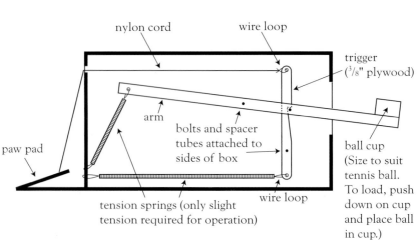

nylon cord

wire loop

trigger
($^3/_8$" plywood)

arm

bolts and spacer tubes attached to sides of box

paw pad

ball cup
(Size to suit tennis ball. To load, push down on cup and place ball in cup.)

tension springs (only slight tension required for operation)

wire loop

Hints on construction

Drill bolt holes through both sides of the body to take the $^1/_2$" (10mm) arm and trigger bolts. Spacer tubes will be needed on both sides of arm and trigger to ensure smooth movement. If more ball height is required, shorten the arm spring slightly.

Keep communicating!— a conclusion

By now you will be well on your way to having a well-trained dog that obeys your every command. You will be using the right form of communication, and you will understand the way your dog thinks.

As we have mentioned at various stages in this book, you should always remember that your dog does not understand human language, and will understand better and respond more correctly if you keep your communication simple. Use simple one-word commands, and reprimand whenever needed with your one-word reprimand. Remember, this is your magic word.

And, as we have emphasized throughout *Train Your Dog the Easy Way*, be sure to reprimand only at the precise moment your dog is doing what you don't want it to do. Praise at the precise moment that it responds correctly.

Be your dog's pack leader by being consistent, and always doing the same thing each time you train it.

If you follow these principles, you can rest assured that you are turning your dog into a well-adjusted creature that will enjoy its life because it is living the way nature intended and the way its ancestors lived—in an ordered environment with a good leader.

As we watch our own two dogs playing and romping in the backyard, we hope you receive as much pleasure from your own dog over the years as they have given us. And we hope sincerely that both of you have enjoyed the process of "training your dog the easy way".

Index

Acknowledgments

Many thanks to:

Both of our families, for all of the support you gave us; thanks also to those who personally helped us in the pursuit of our dream.

Our daughter Donna Ryan, whose beautiful dogs appear in this book.

Liam Crowe and Buddy.

The Laurie family and Cobber.

Kaye Browne and Philip Curro, for your kind (and entertaining!) words.

All the dogs we have trained, or that have crossed our paths over the years. You have taught us so much.

Sylvia and Danny Wilson with Eva and Ceasar.

"The Wind Beneath Our Wings"

*This book is dedicated to the loving memory of
Phillip ("Phil") Hartshorn, trainer of racehorses and
lover of all animals, who was lost to us tragically
in December 1994 in pursuit of his dreams.
His memory will always be an inspiration to us.
Phil will always be the wind beneath our wings.*